Ha! Ha! Ha!
And MUCH More

Maple Tree Press Inc.
51 Front Street East, Suite 200, Toronto, Ontario M5E 1B3
www.mapletreepress.com

Text © 2008 Lyn Thomas
Illustrations © 2008 Dianne Eastman

This book contains material that originally appeared in *Ha! Ha! Ha!* © 2001, and
What? What? What? © 2003.

Distributed in Canada by Raincoast Books
9050 Shaughnessy Street, Vancouver, British Columbia V6P 6E5

Distributed in the United States by Publishers Group West
1700 Fourth Street, Berkeley, California 94710

We acknowledge the financial support of the Canada Council for the Arts, the
Ontario Arts Council, and the Government of Canada through the Book
Publishing Industry Development Program (BPIDP) for our publishing activities.

ONTARIO ARTS COUNCIL
CONSEIL DES ARTS DE L'ONTARIO

Dedication
To my friend Barbara who lives in Melbourne, Australia, and is one of the most amusing people I know. She
made me laugh when we sat together in class and some forty years later she still manages to have me in
stitches—even by email. And I would like to acknowledge all the children in the world who continue to
recycle all the great jokes and Knock! Knocks! that I heard as a child, and still find them funny. *L.T.*

To Harold, for loving laughter. I would also like to recognize the anonymous engravers and illustrators, of
both nineteenth and twentieth centuries, whose fine work has been incorporated into many of the
illustrations in this book. *D.E.*

Cataloguing in Publication Data

Thomas, Lyn, 1949-
    Ha! ha! ha! and much more : the ultimate round-up of jokes, riddles, facts, & puzzles / Lyn Thomas ;
illustrated by Dianne Eastman.

Includes index.
ISBN 978-1-897349-22-9 (bound)   ISBN 978-1-897349-23-6 (pbk.)

1. Riddles, Juvenile. 2. Wit and humor, Juvenile. 3. Puzzles--Juvenile literature.
4. Amusements--Juvenile literature. 5. Curiosities and wonders--Juvenile literature.
I. Eastman, Dianne II. Title.

PN6371.5.T46 2008   j793.73   C2007-906067-6

Library of Congress Control Number: 2007939079

Design & art direction: Dianne Eastman
Illustrations: Dianne Eastman

Printed in Canada

A   B   C   D   E   F

What goes ha, ha, ha, ha, plop?

Someone laughing his head off!

Ha! Ha! Ha!
And MUCH More

The Ultimate Round-up of Jokes, Riddles, Facts, & Puzzles

Written by
LYN THOMAS

Illustrated by
DIANNE EASTMAN

MAPLE
TREE
PRESS

Contents

Get the Good Stuff

Have you heard about the **cross-eyed teacher**? *He couldn't control his pupils*. And what would you get if you crossed a vampire with a teacher? ***A lot of blood tests***! Joking aside, you probably opened this book hoping to find lots of cool jokes and other stuff—some of it **wild**, some of it **crazy**, some of it **scary**, and all of it **amazing**. And that's what you'll find if you read on: the most complete collection of things to **astound** and **amuse** you.

First up check out some **extraordinary animals**, and find out things you would never have guessed about **your own body**. Then **challenge your brain** with some serious bogglers, and discover everything that makes **people unique**. Along the way, move into different kinds of **homes and houses**, explore the depths of the **deepest oceans**, breeze through some **wild weather**, and **fly up** high into the sky. Finally, get the low-down on the most **creative inventions**, and dig into what makes this world wacky, weird, and wonderful. And if that's not enough to have your eyes popping and your head spinning, there are **jokes**, **puzzles**, and **riddles** everywhere you look.

From the **tiniest mouse** to the most giant elephant, from the invention of the first toothbrush to **fish farts**, from circus jokes to hunting for ghosts, from mind-blowing optical illusions to raining cats and dogs, **this book has it all**. Read on and you'll impress your friends and family with your vast knowledge of anything and everything. You'll have them rolling in the aisles quicker than you can say "**Ha! Ha! Ha! And MUCH More**."

Live without a head? Not me!

Why does a tiger have stripes? *So he won't be spotted.* What do you get from a pampered cow? *Spoiled milk.* Why should you walk carefully when it's raining cats and dogs? *You might step in a poodle.* Ok, ok, enough horsing around. From the tiny pygmy marmoset to the giant African elephant and everything in between, the next pages will introduce you to the fastest, strongest, smallest, laziest, and heaviest animals on Earth. You'll also find out why the chicken *really* crossed the road, and why the elephant sat on the marshmallow. Turn the page to read more about amazing animals that will amuse, entertain, and astound you.

Animal Planet

10

Thanks for the Warning, Thumper!

Remember Bambi's bunny friend, Thumper? Like real rabbits, Thumper tapped the ground with his feet. When rabbits sense danger, they thump their enormous feet, probably so the sound will warn others to be on their guard.

11

A Bear-Sized Nap

Grizzly and black bears dig dens in the fall and then go into a dormant period, like hibernation, for 4 to 7 months over the winter. They spend this time in their dens and usually don't eat, urinate, or defecate until they go back out in the spring.

13

And the Award Goes to...

THE SMALLEST

The smallest mammal is the **kitti's hog-nosed bat**. This tiny bat is the size of a bumblebee and weighs less than a penny.

• • •

Pygmy marmosets are the smallest monkeys in the world. Weighing around 113 grams (4 ounces), one of these little monkeys could easily fit in the palm of your hand.

THE FASTEST

The **cheetah** is the world's fastest animal on land, leading the pack at over 110 km/h (70 mph).

• • •

The **peregrine falcon**, a bird, has been clocked diving at around 320 km/h (200 mph). Watch out below!

• • •

Tropical cockroaches are the fastest insects over the ground. They are estimated to move 50 body lengths per second, which is equivalent to a human sprinter running a 100-m (328-ft) race in a little more than a second!

THE LAZIEST

Which animals would wear out the snooze button on their alarm clocks? The **koala** likes to doze for 22 of the 24 hours in a day.

• • •

A **sloth** just wouldn't feel rested without its 20 hours of beauty sleep.

• • •

The **armadillo** and **opossum** aren't far behind, at 19 hours each.

• • •

And your **pet cat** likes to get in 13 hours of zzz's a day to really feel in top form.

Hit and Run

If an elephant charges you at 40 km/h (25 mph), it packs the same wallop as a fully loaded pickup truck going more than 130 km/h (80 mph).

Not Just Any Old Snail

The giant African land snail grows up to 37 cm (15 inches)—that's wider than a large dinner plate—and it's good to eat too! Snail steak anybody?

THE HEAVIEST

The **hippopotamus** can reach a weight of around 4,000 kg (8,900 lbs)—about the same weight as a tractor. But the hippo has to move off the awards platform to make room for an even bigger heavyweight. The heaviest land animal, the **elephant**, can weigh up to a whopping 7,000 kg (15,000 lbs).

LONG LIFERS

Ever wonder how old is old for an elephant? Here are some **average** life spans for some animals:

elephant	60 years
hippopotamus	30–35
grizzly bear	32
horse	20–25
squirrel	8–9
red kangaroo	9–12

But these ages are not as long as these animals *can* live. Here are some amazing, actual recorded ages these animals have reached:

elephant	71
hippopotamus	49
bear	47
horse	50
squirrel	15
kangaroo	23

THE MOST BABIES

A **mouse** can have 6 to 10 litters of up to 12 babies a year (then those babies grow and have babies, too). So one mouse, starting on January 1, can have thousands of descendants by December 31.

BIGGEST EARS

The ears of the **African elephant** can measure nearly 1.8 m (6 ft) high (the height of a tall man) and 1.2 m (4 ft) wide, and they can weigh almost 45 kg (100 lbs). Now that's something to flap about.

Can you guess what this drawing is?

Answer: 4 elephants sniffing an orange.

Why did the chicken cross the road?
To get to the other side.

Why did the cow cross the road?
To see the udder side.

Why did the chicken only cross to the center of the road?
She wanted to lay it on the line.

Why did the *T-rex* cross the road?
Because chickens hadn't evolved yet.

Why did the computer cross the road?
To get to the other site.

Why did the cows cross the road?
To get to the moo-vies.

Why did the dinosaur cross the road?
Because he wasn't a chicken.

Why did the giraffe cross the road?
Because the chicken wasn't around.

Do You Have Any Earplugs?

Does your dog cringe and try to hide under the bed during a thunderstorm? You might too if your ears were as sensitive as a dog's. A dog's hearing is so keen it can hear thunder long before a person can. If those bangs sound loud to you, imagine how they sound to sensitive canine ears.

Does your dog bite?

No.

Ouch! I thought you said your dog doesn't bite.

That's not my dog!

What did the dog say when he sat on the sandpaper?

Ruff! Ruff!

19

🐱 Fluffy's Nine+Lives

Cats have had a colorful history. Ancient Egyptians worshipped them. They even mummified cats when they died—the same honor bestowed on Pharaohs. By the second century, cats had become popular in Europe as well. But around 1300, trouble started for the cat. People came to believe that cats were associated with evil and witches. Soon cats were almost extinct in Europe. Then the Black Death plague struck. Borne by disease-carrying rats, this devasting disease rapidly spread across the continent. Millions of people died. Luckily for our feline friends, people saw how valuable cats are when it comes to keeping down the rodent population. Seems like cats have earned their current status as beloved household pets.

Animals Just Want to Have Fun

Like us, animals seem to like to play and have fun, especially baby animals. Scientists believe that aside from sheer enjoyment, playing together is a form of bonding with their fellow animals. Also, some kinds of play help young animals to grow strong and to learn important survival skills, such as pouncing on prey to become good hunters.

Animal Facts

Animal Phrases

We use animal phrases, like "it's raining cats and dogs," all the time. Here are two more:

GET YOUR GOAT! If someone is making you angry, you might say they are "getting your goat." Actually, it originally was "get your goad." A goad is a cattle prod, used to poke animals to make them hurry up or move.

HAPPY AS A CLAM. When something great happens to you, you feel "happy as a clam." The original phrase is actually "happy as a clam at high tide." Since clam diggers can only wade into the seawater and dig for clams in the sand at low tide, clams are happy and safe from capture at high tide.

Woof? Woof?

Everybody knows that when a dog barks it says Woof! Right? Well, not exactly. A French dog would probably sound the same to you as an English one does, but the way the noises are written in different languages can be fun to look at. A Russian dog, for instance, says Gaf! And a Czech dog says Haf! In Finland, dogs say How! And in Denmark it's Vov! Here are some other animal sounds:

	ENGLISH	FRENCH	SPANISH
DOG	Woof!	Oua!	Gauff!
CAT	Meow!	Miaou!	Miau!
COW	Moo!	Meu!	Moou!

Moou!

You speak Spanish well.

Mooo-chas gracias!

A Fishing Cat?

It's true! Most cats hate water, but the Asian fishing cat is a strong swimmer—even underwater! It does catch fish, but is believed to eat mostly snakes, frogs, and crustaceons.

Climbing Cat

In 1950 a four-month-old kitten followed mountaineers to the top of the Matterhorn in the Alps. It climbed the 4,000 m (14,000 ft) trek in stages, but got a break on the way down when it hitched a ride in a mountain guide's backpack.

Animals New, Very Old, and Somewhere in Between

DINOS FOR DINNER

Next time you bite into a piece of fried **chicken**, consider that you may be eating a cousin of the mighty *T-rex*. It is the general belief of paleontologists, who collect evidence of the past, that dinosaur descendants survive to this day—in the form of birds! Fossils of feathered dinosaurs, found in a rich fossil bed in China, indicate a close evolutionary connection.

Prehistoric Grindstones
There's another way some dinosaurs were like chickens—they had a hard time digesting their food, so they swallowed stones to help grind it up.

MONKEY BUSINESS

A new monkey, the **dwarf marmoset**—measuring just 15 cm (6 inches) long, with a 22 cm (9 inch) tail—has been discovered living in the Brazilian Amazon region. Amazingly, this little creature was found in a forest only a short way from a very heavily populated city. If these little monkeys have been living so close, but unnoticed for so long, imagine what species might yet be found in remote rainforests.

Tiny monkeys—the size of a human thumb—once existed, as proved by the fossilized remains found in a limestone quarry in the Jiangsu province of China. The remains were found in the regurgitated, fossilized food of owls...that lost their lunch at least forty-five million years ago!

WHAT'S A ZORILLA?

No, it's not a cross between a zebra and a gorilla. Also known as the **striped polecat**, it's an African animal that looks a lot like a skunk. Although skunks and zorillas do not belong to the same species, they don't just look alike—they stink alike too. Both have scent glands they use in defense against other animals. Pew!

When Mammoths Ruled the Earth

Mammoths probably evolved about 2 million years back, and they disappeared from the Earth about 10,000 years ago. Although they resembled elephants, they were up to 4.5 m (15 ft) tall, about the height of a one-story house.

What kind of key opens a banana?

A monkey.

Why are elephants wrinkled?
Would you like to try to iron one?

Why did the woman want an elephant instead of a car?
The elephant had a bigger trunk.

What did the elephant do when he broke his toe and couldn't walk?
He called a toe truck.

What do you do with a green elephant?
Wait for it to get ripe.

What's gray and squirts jam at you?
An elephant eating a doughnut.

What's large and bright purple?
An elephant holding its breath.

What has a long trunk and is found on the North Pole?
A lost elephant.

What do you get when you cross an elephant with peanut butter?
Either an elephant that sticks to the roof of your mouth or peanut butter that never forgets.

How do you hide an elephant?
Paint its tusks yellow and put it in a banana tree.

What do you give an elephant with big feet?
Lots of room.

What should you do if you see a naked elephant in a swimming pool?
Give him back his trunks.

Why can't two elephants go swimming at the same time?
They've only got one pair of trunks between them.

How does an elephant get down from a tree?
It sits on a leaf and waits for fall.

Ear This !

The ears of the African elephant can measure nearly 2m (6 ft) high—and can weigh almost 45 kg. (100 lbs)! They don't just look good. They help an elephant keep its cool, too. When elephants flap their ears, it helps the extra blood vessels in their ears release heat. And those big ears make good fans, too.

**What do elephants take
when they go away on
a long trip?**
Their trunks.

**Why do elephants paint
their toenails red?**
So they can hide in a straw-
berry patch.

**What did the grape say
to the elephant?**
Nothing, grapes can't talk.

**How can you tell that
an elephant has been
in your refrigerator?**
Look for footprints in the
butter.

**Why can't elephants
drive cars?**
Their feet are too big for
the pedals.

**Why do elephants wear
green hats?**
So they can blend into the
crowds on St. Patrick's Day.

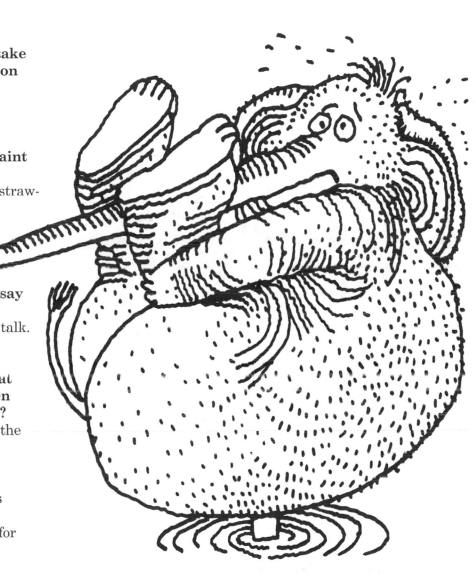

**Why did the elephant sit
on the marshmallow?**
It didn't want to fall into
the hot chocolate.

Why can't you play games in the jungle?
Because there's always gonna be a cheetah.

What has stripes and sixteen wheels?
A zebra wearing roller skates.

What's black and white and eats like a horse?
A zebra.

What monkey is always exploding?
A ba-boom.

What do snakes do after a fight?
Hiss and make up.

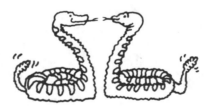

What's a monkey's favorite Christmas song?
Jungle bells.

What do you call a hippopotamus with the measles?

A hippo-spotty-mus.

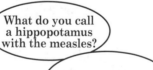

Why can't you play jokes on snakes?
You can't pull their legs!

What do you do if a 6-ton gorilla tells you a joke?
You laugh ...very loudly!

Why do lions eat raw meat?
They don't know how to cook.

What do you call a lion that's eaten your dad's sister?
An aunt-eater.

Drooling Crocs!

Have you ever looked closely at a crocodile's jaws? Probably not . . . or you wouldn't be here to read this! But if you examine a photograph of a crocodile, you'll see that they have huge mouths and lots of teeth, but they don't have any lips. Without lips to seal them shut, their mouths leak when they're closed. How embarrassing!

What's invisible and smells like banana?
A gorilla's burp.

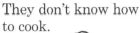

How do you stop a cobra from striking?

unfair

Pay it a decent wage.

more $

Why do gorillas have such large nostrils?
Because they have such big fingers.

Mammal Mania

When is a bear not a bear? When it's a koala. A koala is a marsupial, which is a mammal with a pouch, like a kangaroo.

What do American buffaloes and bison have in common? Everything! They are the same animal. The American buffalo is not a buffalo at all, but a bison.

Why does the three-toed sloth look green? It hangs around in the damp jungles of South America and green algae grows on its fur!

Why won't your cat do tricks? Unlike dogs, whose relatives in the wild live in packs and have to work together, cats have never learned to take orders. Wild cats are mostly solitary and independent. But then, you knew your cat had a mind of its own, didn't you?

Have you ever noticed that all dogs—except the chow-chow —have black lips? This stops them getting sunburned. The chow-chow is the only dog with blue lips.

Why do elephants flap their ears? No, they're not waving hello. Elephant ears are like giant radiators, full of blood vessels, so when an elephant flaps its ears it is really staying cool!

Love Is Blind
Good thing naked mole-rats are almost blind, because they aren't what most would call pretty. But each colony has a beauty—the Queen—who can have more than one mate.

Scavengers, or animals that feed on dead or injured animals, clean the Earth of organic garbage. Here are some animals on that necessary team—and some might surprise you!

Bears often follow ravens in order to find dead fish to eat. Alaskan brown bears feed on dead seals, walruses and whales that have floated ashore.

Hyenas hunt and scavenge in packs, and so do **jackals**. In hungry times, hyenas will eat jackals, but when there's plenty of food around, you might see both these kinds of wild dogs scavenging together.

Leopards and **lions** will scavenge when their hunting is unsuccessful.

Raccoons eat garbage from dumps and cans, especially if it smells of chicken or fish.

Rats will eat almost anything.

> **Great dinner! But I don't have a scent.**

> **I don't have a buck to my name.**

> **That's OK, just put it on my bill.**

A Nose for Death
Many birds don't have a very good sense of smell. But the turkey vulture, flying high in the sky, finds dead animal flesh simply by smell.

Cowabunga!

How many stomachs does a cow have? Only one, just like we do, except there are four compartments in a cow's stomach. These come in handy because, on average, a cow eats about 36 kgs (80 lbs.) of food a day!

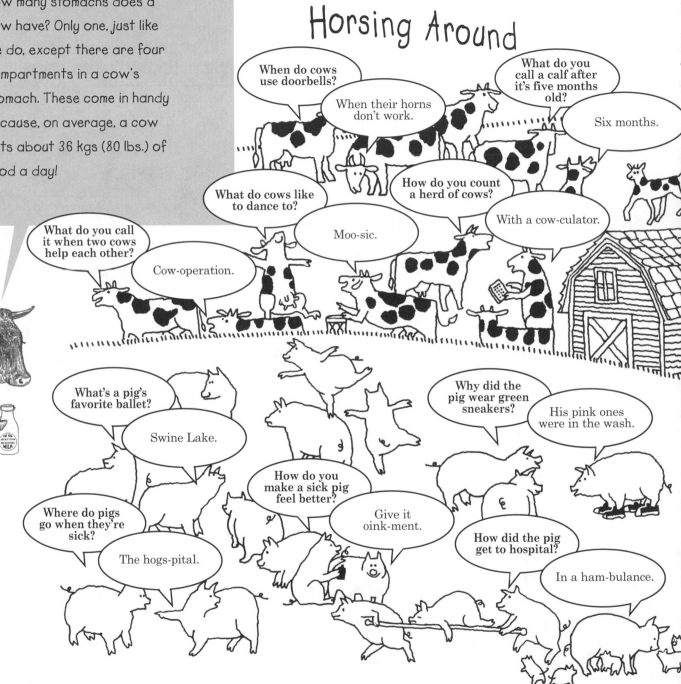

Horsing Around

When do cows use doorbells?

When their horns don't work.

What do you call a calf after it's five months old?

Six months.

What do cows like to dance to?

Moo-sic.

How do you count a herd of cows?

With a cow-culator.

What do you call it when two cows help each other?

Cow-operation.

What's a pig's favorite ballet?

Swine Lake.

Why did the pig wear green sneakers?

His pink ones were in the wash.

How do you make a sick pig feel better?

Give it oink-ment.

Where do pigs go when they're sick?

The hogs-pital.

How did the pig get to hospital?

In a ham-bulance.

35

Animal Families

*Lots of animals, insects, amphibians and reptiles never meet their parents.
And if baby animals are raised by a parent it is usually the mother.
But step up and meet some interesting animal fathers.*

● ● ●

Most male ducks live alone, but the **ruddy duck** of
North America helps care for his young.

● ● ●

A father **cockroach** eats bird droppings to obtain precious
nitrogen, which he carries back to feed his young.

● ● ●

The male **darwin's frog** hatches eggs in a pouch in his
mouth. He can eat and continue about his daily life
until the tadpoles become tiny frogs and leap out of his
mouth to begin life alone.

● ● ●

A **marmoset** dad takes care of his baby monkeys as
soon as they are born. He cleans them, takes them to
their mother for nursing, and even feeds them when
they start eating solid food.

● ● ●

Wolves, like us, like to live as a family. After a mother wolf has given
birth to her pups, the dad will bring food for the mom and cubs. He
will be outside guarding the den until they are old enough to begin
playing and learning survival skills, which he will teach them.

● ● ●

As soon as the female **midwife toad** lays her eggs, the male wraps
strings of them around his back legs to guard them. When the eggs
are ready to hatch, he spreads them over the surface of the water. Out
pop the tadpoles and away paddles dad.

Mighty Mom
Most insects lay eggs, then leave
them to hatch by themselves. But
the female earwig sticks around to
protect her young—even against
such large enemies as spiders
and birds.

36

People have come up with funny names to describe groups of animals.
Here are some interesting ones:

A mischief of mice
A congregation of alligators
A sloth of bears
A colony of beavers
A murder of crows
An unkindness of ravens
An army of frogs
A gaggle of geese
A swarm of grasshoppers
A bloat of hippos
A charm of hummingbirds
A smack of jellyfish
A mob of kangaroos
A leap of leopards
A pride of lions
A troop of monkeys
A parliament of owls
A company of parrots
A crash of rhinos
A shiver of sharks
A pod of whales

What did the porcupine say to the cactus?

Is that you, Mommy?

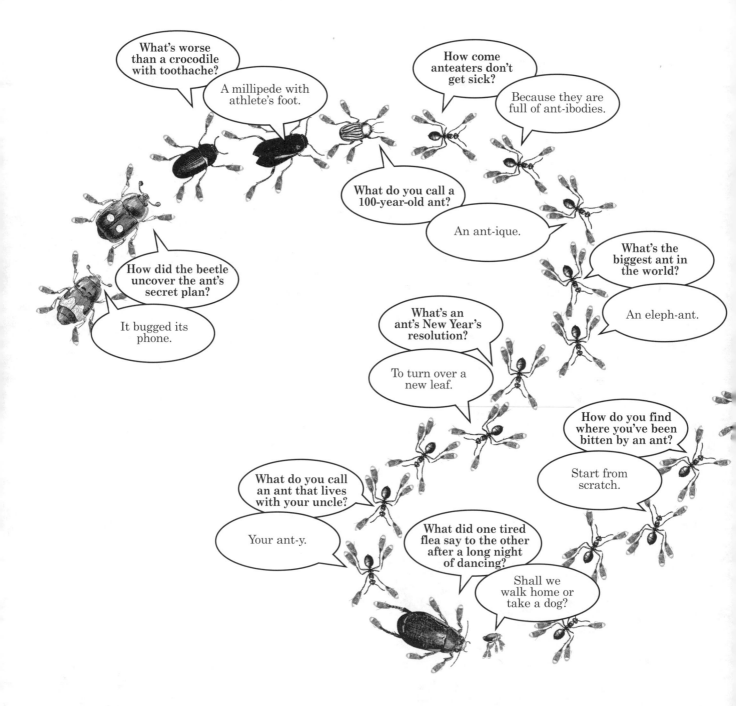

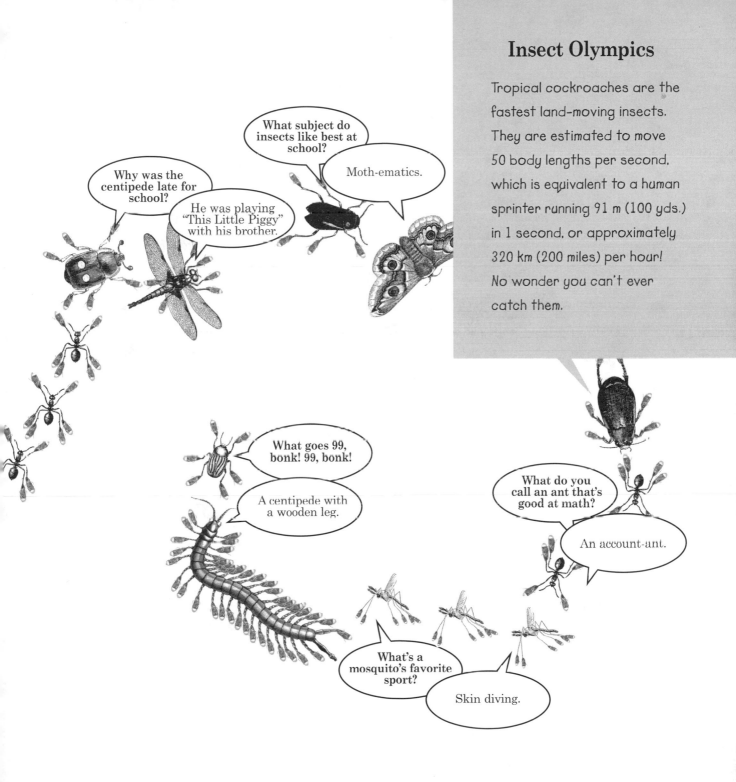

Insect Olympics

Tropical cockroaches are the fastest land-moving insects. They are estimated to move 50 body lengths per second, which is equivalent to a human sprinter running 91 m (100 yds.) in 1 second, or approximately 320 km (200 miles) per hour! No wonder you can't ever catch them.

39

Creepy Crawlies

SPIDEY SENSES AND MORE

The poisonous female **black widow spider** often eats her mate after mating, which explains the name.

• • •

Spiders are voracious predators. All the insects eaten by spiders in one year would weigh more than all the people on Earth.

• • •

Spiders can re-grow missing legs or parts of legs.

• • •

A spider usually stays in a web only one to two days before moving on to making another one.

• • •

There are about 800 known species of tarantula in the world and they are found in every country except Antarctica.

• • •

The bite of a tarantula is venomous but, according to scientists, they rarely bite people and there is no recorded evidence of a person dying from a tarantula bite.

SPIDER MAN

Not everyone considers the **tarantula** a beautiful and timid creature, but a doctor in Scotland does. He has around 2,000 of them, including the goliath birdeater from South America. This spider's name isn't really correct, as a birdeater is much more likely to eat rodents and frogs that accidentally find their way into its underground homes. The doctor is especially fond of one goliath he has reared—with a leg span of 28 cm (11 inches) and weight around 170 g (6 oz), it must be the undisputed heavyweight champion of spiders!

HEY, CUCARACHA!

There are about 3,500 species of **cockroaches**. They even live at the North and South Poles.

• • •

The world's largest cockroach lives in South America, is about 15 cm (6 inches) long, and has a 30 cm (1 ft) wingspan, which is about the size of a frisbee. Imagine seeing that flying towards you!

• • •

A cockroach can live for up to a week without a head. Yuck.

Flexing Your Muscles...All Day
Caterpillars have more than 4,000 muscles—that's about seven times as many as you have!

Good Help Is Hard to Find
Amazon ants can't do anything but fight, so they steal the larvae of other ants and raise them to do everything else. The servant ants feed the Amazon ants, and even build homes for them.

Mexican Bean Dance
Have you ever seen a Mexican jumping bean? The seed of a shrub, it has an insect larva inside. When you hold it, the warmth from your hand makes the larva start to move around, making the bean jump and dance.

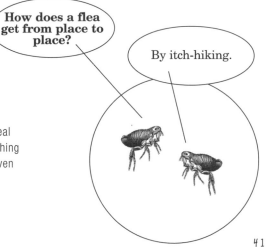

How does a flea get from place to place?

By itch-hiking.

41

Mosquito's Best Friend

Do mosquitoes think you're particularly tasty? Some believe that mosquitoes are more attracted to some people's blood than others. One theory is that it might have something to do with the amount of carbon dioxide a person's skin releases. Others believe it's the warmth and wetness of the skin that's appealing. And there are those who believe that everyone gets bitten equally, but not everyone reacts the same way.

Slither, Sneak, Slide, Splash!

It can run at scary speed on short legs, has a poisonous bite, reaches more than 3 m (10 ft) in length and comes from the island of Komodo. Although it's called a dragon, the **Komodo dragon** is really just an enormous lizard.

● ● ●

A **chameleon** can move its eyes in two different directions at the same time.

● ● ●

The **desert tortoise** will dig huge burrows to seek relief from the intense heat.

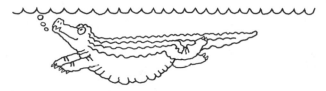

An adult **crocodile** will swallow up to 5 kg (11 lbs) of stones. Scientists think the extra weight in its stomach might help keep the croc underwater when it's swimming.

● ● ●

Unlike **snakes**, which shed their skin all at once when they molt, **crocodiles** shed their scales individually.

● ● ●

You've heard of Chinese dragons? How about a **Chinese alligator**? It's only about half the size of its American cousin, growing to a length of about 2 m (6 ½ ft). Which is quite big enough, thank you.

● ● ●

70 million years ago **turtles** used to be the size of small cars.

● ● ●

A species of **frog** is known to burrow into the frozen mud of the Arctic. But you don't need a microwave oven to defrost these frogs' legs—when the weather gets warmer, the frogs thaw out all by themselves.

● ● ●

One **frog** in Ecuador is known to give off a pain-killing chemical scientists believe is 200 times more powerful than the strongest pain-killer drugs.

When some **lizards** need to escape from an enemy they drop their tails and run! Usually the enemy is so confused it forgets all about the lizard. New tails grow later.

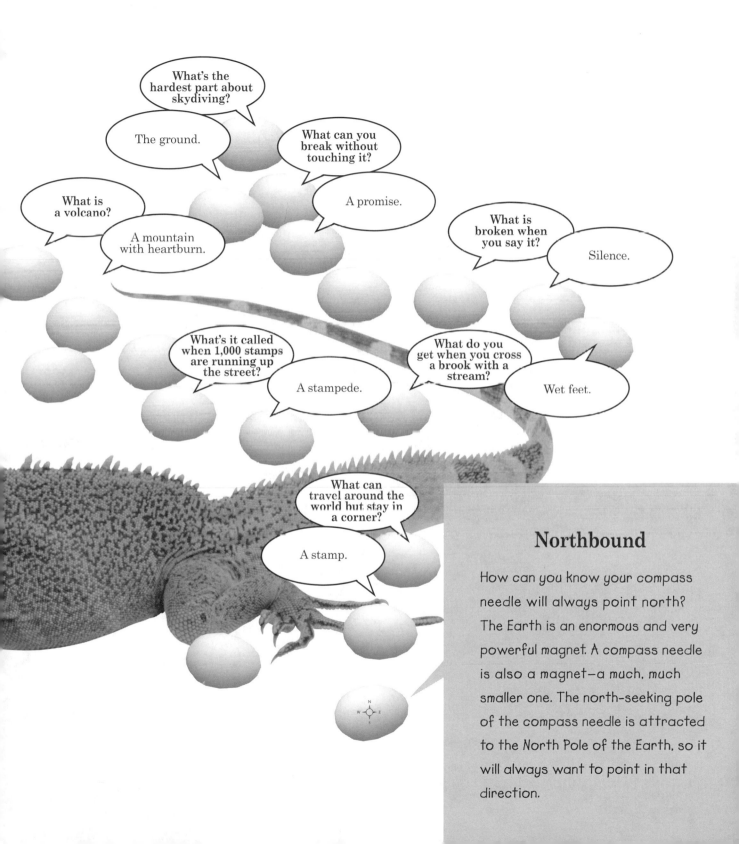

Northbound

How can you know your compass needle will always point north? The Earth is an enormous and very powerful magnet. A compass needle is also a magnet—a much, much smaller one. The north-seeking pole of the compass needle is attracted to the North Pole of the Earth, so it will always want to point in that direction.

Where do frogs fly their flags?
Up tad-poles.

Where do tadpoles change into frogs?
In the croak-room.

Where does a frog go to get glasses?
The hop-tometrist.

What happened to the frog's car when it was illegally parked?
It got toad.

Why did the frog croak?
It ate a poisonous fly.

What does a frog look like when it has a broken leg?
Unhoppy.

What goes into the water green but comes out blue?
A frog on a cold day.

What do you get when you cross a frog with a rabbit?
A rabbit that says "ribbit."

What's green and loud and can be heard for miles?
A frog horn.

What's a frog's favorite year?
Leap year.

Now That's a Great Mom!

One kind of poison dart frog goes to great heights for her young. Once the tadpoles are hatched, she carries them from the forest floor to the top of the trees, where she deposits them in the little pools of water that collect in the leaves of certain trees. It's a tough climb, but these are devoted moms.

Why did the
bee hum?

It forgot the
words.

hmmmmmm hmmmmm hmmm hmmmmmmmmm hmmmm hmmm hmmm

**Why don't you ever see an
unhappy frog?**
They eat whatever
bugs them.

Did you hear about the optician who fell into a lens grinder? *He made a spectacle of himself.* What kind of physician works on a cruise liner? *A dry doc.* What do you get if you have strep throat on Friday? *Saturday night fever.* Your body is made up of around 100 billion tiny living cells—there are way more cells in one human being than jokes in this book! Keep reading to find out how many hairs are on your head, which part of your body is the size of a football, and how much a human eyeball weighs. Get an inside look at some of the awesome things you—and your body—do everyday.

Body Language

Nothing but Skin and Bones... and Hair

THE SKINNY ON SKIN

The skin is the body's largest organ, weighing 2 to 4.5 kg (5–10 lbs).

• • •

Your skin is germ-proof, waterproof, and stretchy, and it rejuvenates itself.

• • •

We lose and replace our outer skin about every 27 days. Depending on how long you live, you could have up to 1,000 new outer skins in your lifetime.

• • •

We don't really know if scratching stops an itch. If not, then at least it is a stronger sensation that distracts your attention from the annoying itch. Aaaah!

A CLEAN SWEEP

Ever wondered where the dust in your house comes from? Aside from stuff like dirt and fluff, a lot of it is probably your skin. An average person sheds about 600,000 particles of skin every hour. That works out to about 0.64 kg (1.5 lbs) a year, or about 48 kg (100 lbs) in a lifetime. Add to that the 1.5 million hairs you lose over a lifetime—about 45 to 60 a day—and you've got some giant dust bunnies!

BONING UP

Around 206 bones keep an adult upright, along with muscles and ligaments.

• • •

Did you know that a baby is born with around 350 bones? As we grow, lots of little bones grow together to form larger bones.

• • •

How many bones are in your head? One, right? Wrong! The helmet of bone that protects your brain is actually seven bones that fit together like the pieces of a jigsaw puzzle.

HAIR, THERE, AND EVERYWHERE

Whether their hair is long or short, most people have about 100,000 hairs on their head.

• • •

If you twisted a rope out of 1,000 hairs, it could lift up two or three kids at once. Now that's strong!

I Was a Teenage Hairball

Once you get through the hairy and sweaty teen years, you end up with more than 2 million sweat glands and about 5 million hairs on your body.

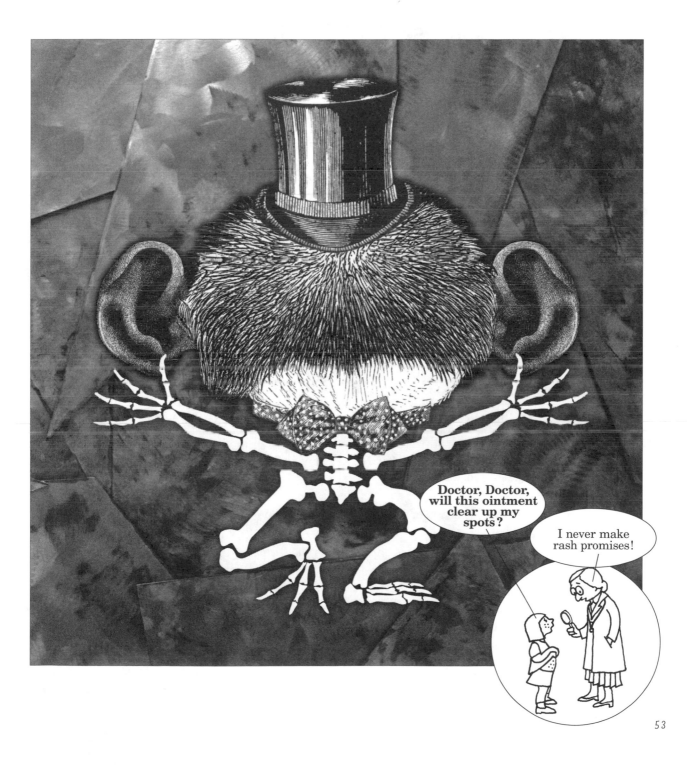

53

Muscles to the Max

The most powerful muscle in your whole body is attached to your head—your jaw muscle. Muscles get stronger by being used, and your jaw muscle gets a lot of exercise by moving your jawbone up and down as you talk, chew, yawn, laugh, and grind your teeth.

● ● ●

Did you know that fingers don't have muscles? They move by very strong ligaments that are attached to your hands and forearms.

Why does it hurt when you laugh really hard? When someone tells you a funny joke, you tense up your stomach muscles, and the muscle under your lungs (your diaphragm) pumps up and down. Eventually you end up with over-exercised muscles—and they hurt!

● ● ●

When you walk, you use around 200 muscles—about ⅓ of all the muscles in your body.

● ● ●

About 43% of a man's weight is muscle, and 36% of a woman's.

● ● ●

You feel aching deltoids and triceps in your arms. But if someone says their gluteus maximus aches, they have a pain in the bum!

● ● ●

Did you know that you can move your tongue in just about every direction? There are no bones to stop the muscles from moving every which way.

This is me smiling.

Knock knock.
Who's there?
Goliath.
Goliath who?
**Goliath down.
You looketh tired.**

Humans have more facial muscles than any other animal,
and can make around 7,000 different expressions.

56

The Heart of the Matter

The heart is a hollow muscle, and it isn't heart-shaped at all. It sits in the middle of your chest and pumps blood around the body, supplying all the cells and muscles with oxygen and nutrients.

● ● ●

The left hand side of your heart pumps the blood around your body, but the right pumps blood just to your lungs.

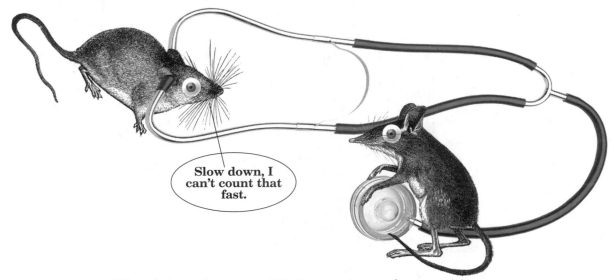

Slow down, I can't count that fast.

Although it can beat up to 200 times a minute when exercising or stressed, an adult heart usually beats between 60 and 80 times a minute. Compare this with a baby's heart, which beats about 130 times a minute. A mouse's heart races at about 600 or 700 times a minute; an elephant has a pulse of 25. The smaller the heart, the faster it beats.

Lub-dub, Lub-dub

When you listen to your heartbeat, what you really hear is the sound of your heart valves closing. The beat itself is a silent contraction of the muscles.

Prrrr, prrr, prrr...prrressure down yet?

3,000 Round-Trip Tickets
A blood cell travels through the circulatory system about 3,000 times before being replaced.

PETS ARE GOOD FOR YOU

If you have a pet, there is a good chance that your **blood pressure** is lower. Often animals, particularly cats and dogs, are pets in homes for older or sick people. When a human touches and strokes an animal, the sensation of calm helps relax them and can lower their blood pressure at the same time.

BLOOD IS THICKER THAN WATER

While resting, an adult heart pushes about 5.7 liters (1.5 gallons) of blood through the whole body every minute, taking oxygen gas from the lungs to the rest of the body. That comes to more than 213 million liters (50 million gallons) in an average life span—enough blood to fill 18 Olympic swimming pools.

Blood is made up of red blood cells that carry oxygen, white blood cells that help fight germs, and platelets that help the body heal itself—all swimming in plasma, which is the liquid part of the blood.

Doctor, Doctor, I'm boiling up!

Just simmer down!

What did the left hand say to the right hand?
How does it feel to always be right?

What did one eye say to the other?
Between you and me, something smells.

What do you lose every time you stand up?
Your lap.

What goes up but never comes down?
Your age.

What did one ear say to the other ear?
Hear! Hear!

What can you hold in your right hand but not in your left hand?
Your left elbow.

What kind of button can't you unbutton?
A belly button.

What runs but doesn't have legs?
Your nose.

Fascinating Fingernails

Bet you didn't know that your fingernails and toenails grow faster in the summer than in the winter. But all through the year fingernails grow more quickly than toenails. Nobody knows why for sure, but it may be because we use our fingers and fingernails more than our toenails.

61

The Inner You

Which part of your body is the size of a football? It's one of your lungs.

• • •

Without you even thinking about it, you breathe around 16 times a minute. In an average lifetime, that's about 600 million breaths.

• • •

Each day about 18 m³ (18.5 cubic yards) of air are cleaned, moistened, and warmed by the air passages in your lungs. With that much air, you could fill up around 300 balloons!

• • •

What are **crepitations**? Strange sea monsters? No, it's what doctors call the noise they hear in the lungs of people who are sick. It's a crackling sound that could identify an illness like pneumonia.

The liver is the body's chemical factory for processing the blood. It does more than 500 jobs, including storing vitamins A and D, straining out worn-out blood cells and poisons, and producing bile for digestion.

Kidneys filter blood and remove waste.

What's **borborygmi**? Listen—it sounds like what it is, the noise that comes from your tummy when you're hungry. The growling sound is caused by digestive juices—with no food to act on, they just splash and gurgle around in there. Borborygmi, borborygmi....

• • •

Burps are swallowed air. Maybe you've taken gulps of air while eating, or there's lots of air in whatever you swallowed—for example, the carbon dioxide that makes the bubbles in soda—that gets released in the stomach. So, the air comes up, bubbles over the back of the throat, and—oops, excuse me!

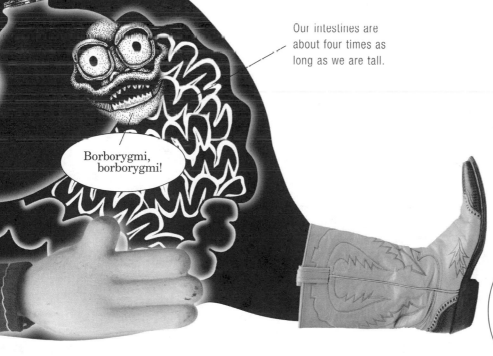

Our intestines are about four times as long as we are tall.

Borborygmi, borborygmi!

A man walks into a doctor's office. He has a cucumber up his nose, a carrot in his left ear, and a banana in his right ear. "What's the matter with me, Doctor?" he asks. "You're not eating properly," replies the doctor.

Eyes, Ears, Mouth, and Nose

EYE WONDER WHY...

Why do babies seem so wide-eyed when they look at the world? The size of a baby's eye is almost the same as it will be when the baby grows up. It just looks bigger inside a smaller face.

• • •

A **human eyeball** weighs about 28 grams (1 ounce) and has a diameter of about 2.5 cm (1 inch). That's as big as the space across the face of a quarter.

THE NOSE KNOWS

An average nose can tell the difference between as many as 4,000 to 10,000 different odors. A perfume expert can smell up to about 30,000 different scents.

• • •

A **sneeze** can produce wind speeds as great as a hurricane!

VERY TASTY

*Stick your tongue out and look in the mirror. Can you see those tiny lumps? They are your **taste buds**, and your tongue has about 10,000 of them.*

Each taste bud is about ⅟₃₀ mm (1/750 inches) in diameter and twice as long. Under a microscope the buds look like miniature rosebuds in bloom.

• • •

Taste buds are constantly being renewed, since each one lasts only about ten days.

• • •

You have taste buds on your tongue, the roof of your mouth, and your throat.

• • •

We lose our taste buds as we get older, so you have more of them than an adult does.

EAR YE, EAR YE!

Where do you find **hammers, canals, stirrups,** and **anvils**? If you're looking in a carpenter's workshop, you're in the wrong place. Look no further than yourself—these are all part of a human ear.

• • •

You might think that the **wax** and **hairs** in your ears are a bit yucky, but without them germs wouldn't be trapped. Your nose contains hair for the same reason.

• • •

Ever wondered why you get **dizzy** when you spin around? There's liquid in your inner ear that spins around with you. When you stop the spinning, the liquid doesn't—and gives you a dizzy sensation.

CHOMPING ALONG

What do trees and teeth have in common? Another name for the baby teeth we drop is "deciduous," the same name for trees that drop their leaves in fall.

Chew on This
Teeth are the hardest part of your body.

I Think... I Know... What I Feel

Scientists know that **handedness** (whether you favor your right or left hand for everyday actions) is decided in the brain. Only a few people are ambidextrous, which means they can use either hand to do the same task, like writing or throwing. Other people are mixed-handed—they can do different tasks with different hands.

Yawn Until You Cry

Why do you cry when you're laughing really hard? Or when you yawn? Your squeezed-up face puts pressure on the tear glands. If the glands are full, tears will drop out.

IT'S ALL IN YOUR HEAD

Right now, you have around 13 or 14 million **nerve cells**, called neurons, in you brain and each cell holds about 10,000 bits of information. During a lifetime of 70 or so years, a person's memory banks hold at least 100 trillion—that's 100,000,000,000,000—bits of information.

• • •

The only cells in the body that are not replaced are those in the brain. Since taking drugs and drinking alcohol kills brain cells, you've got to wonder—can you afford to lose them?

My head's full. No more information, please.

When you are really scared of something, you have a **phobia**. There are hundreds of different phobias, and their names don't always mean what they seem to. If you have melissophobia, you won't run scared from anyone named Melissa—you suffer from a fear of bees! You might not think that the things listed here are scary, but some people do, and that's why they're phobias. Match the phobias to the scary—or not-so-scary—things, then turn the page upside-down to check:

1. Achluophobia	a) fear of fish
2. Ceraunophobia	b) fear of vegetables
3. Dendrophobia	c) fear of knees
4. Genuphobia	d) fear of slime
5. Glossophobia	e) fear of worms
6. Ichthyophobia	f) fear of thunder
7. Lachanophobia	g) fear of snakes
8. Myxophobia	h) fear of darkness
9. Ophidiophobia	i) fear of speaking in public
10. Scoleciphobia	j) fear of trees

Who, me? Scared?

Answers: 1, h; 2, f; 3, j; 4, c; 5, i; 6, a; 7, b; 8, d; 9, g; 10, e.

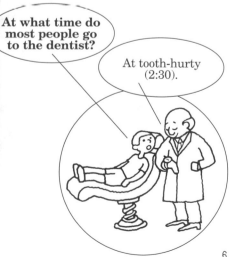

At what time do most people go to the dentist?

At tooth-hurty (2:30).

If two is company and three's a crowd, what's four and five? *Nine!* If you have it, you want to share it. If you share it, you don't have it. What is it? *A secret!* What's black and white and read all over? *These awesome pages of brain bogglers, of course!* Test your brain and use your thinking skills on the next few pages by figuring out some of the toughest brain busters this side of the moon.

Brain Bogglers

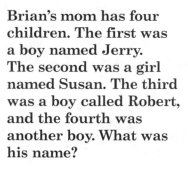

The Jones family built a house, only to find that all four walls faced south. When they were finished building, they looked out the window and saw a bear. What color was the bear?

Mary's sister has some strange likes and dislikes. She'll buy paste but not glue; she'll eat in a deli but not a cafe; she'll ride in a cab but never a taxi. Try to figure out why she likes and dislikes these things.

Brian's mom has four children. The first was a boy named Jerry. The second was a girl named Susan. The third was a boy called Robert, and the fourth was another boy. What was his name?

Answer: White. The house must have been built on the North Pole, as this is the only point on Earth where all four walls of the house could face south. Therefore, the bear was a white polar bear.

Answer: Mary's sister only likes things whose names contain two letters in alphabetical order, for example, table, paste, and deli.

Answer: Brian.

Duncan decides to take a bath and starts filling his tub. When the water reaches the top he tries to turn off the tap but it falls off. The bathroom's windows don't open and the door closes with an airtight seal. The room begins to fill up with water. Duncan can't get the door open. How does he save himself?

Uh, oh! You made Sook Yin laugh, and now everyone has the giggles. Use the clues below to figure out how long Sook Yin laughed.

•Sook Yin laughed twice as long as Patrick.
•Patrick laughed three times as long as Taryn.
•Taryn laughed as long as Emeka did.
•Emeka laughed twice as long as Jack.
•Jack laughed for half a minute.

Your Amazing Brain

If all the nerve connections in one brain were stretched out and placed end to end, they would be long enough to go around the Earth several times! And if it were possible to convert one human brain's metabolism into energy, it would equal a 20 watt lightbulb. If all the brains in the world were converted, that would be enough energy to power around 15 big cities. Now that's brain power!

Answer: All he has to do is pull the plug so the tub can drain.

Answer: Sook Yin laughed for 6 minutes.

71

Susan and Sheila have the same parents, look exactly alike, and are the same age. But they are not twins. How is this possible?

If it takes five people one day to dig up a field, how long will it take ten people to dig up the same field?

Patty was asked how many ducks she had. She answered, "As they ran down the path, I saw one duck in front of two ducks, a duck behind two ducks, and a duck between two ducks." How many ducks did Patty have?

Answer: Susan, Sheila, and their sister Sandra are triplets.

Answer: No time at all! The field has already been dug up.

Answer: Three. The ducks were waddling down the path in single file.

Ouch!

Have you ever wondered why it hurts when someone pulls your hair, but you don't feel anything when someone cuts it? That's because your hair that's grown out is made of dead cells. But your hair under your scalp is alive, and it's attached to nerves. When it's pulled the nerves send a "pain" message to your brain.

A teacher left a first prize ribbon on his desk when he left the classroom. When he returned a few minutes later the ribbon was gone. He called the three students who had been in the room, and asked them if they'd seen it. The first said she'd seen it but left it where it was. The second said he'd seen it too. He said he was worried that it might blow away because the window was open, so he put it under a book on the desk. The third student said she'd seen it and was also worried that it might go missing, so she placed it between pages 53 and 54 of the book. The teacher looked, but it wasn't there. Which of the three students was lying, and how did the teacher know?

Answer: The third. It would be impossible to put anything between pages 53 and 54. In a book, odd pages always fall on the right and even pages on the left, so 53 and 54 couldn't be facing each other, they would be back-to-back. The student could have put the note between pages 52 and 53, or 54 and 55, but not 53 and 54.

1

Who is this person? It is not my sister, nor my brother, but it is a child of my father and mother.

2

If your aunt's brother is not your uncle, then who is he?

3

Who is your father's sister's sister-in-law?

4

I have eyes but cannot see. I have ears but cannot hear. I have lips but cannot speak. I will always look the same. Nothing will ever change me. What am I?

5

I have lived one year. I have lived hundreds of years. I am seen in nearly every part of the world. I live near mountains, near the sea, near the roads and plains. I am a life force. Without me the world will be bare.

6

What doesn't get any wetter no matter how much it rains?

7

If a cat can jump 5 feet in the air, then why can't it jump through a 2-foot high window?

8

What has a mouth but doesn't eat, a bank without money, a bed but doesn't sleep, and waves but has no hands?

9

David's father has three sons: Snap, Crackle, and _____?

10

You're a bus driver on your bus route. At the first stop, three girls with blonde hair get on, while a man eating an ice cream cone gets off. At the second stop, five boys who just won their baseball game, and a woman with a yellow-polka-dot dress pay the fee and enter the bus; nobody gets off. At the third stop, a man carrying a monkey exits the bus. Nobody new joins the ride. What's the bus driver's name?

11

A bus driver is going up a one-way street the wrong way. Halfway down the street he gets spotted by a police officer, and waves hello to him. If the bus driver is going down a one-way street the wrong way, why does the police officer not pull him over and give him a ticket?

Space Invader

Everyone has it, but yours might be different from your friend's or your brother's, or sister's. What is it? Personal space. That's the space immediately around you. If someone else comes into it, it makes you feel uncomfortable. But your personal space shrinks and grows depending on whom you're with. If it's someone you trust, your personal space will be smaller. For strangers, it grows!

Can you name ten parts of the body that are spelled with only three letters?

There are two coins on the table totaling 35 cents. One of them is not a quarter. What are the coins?

A boy and his father were driving in a car during a snowstorm when the car crashed. Both were injured and had to be rushed into surgery. The surgeon walked into the boy's operating room, looked at the patient and said, "I can't operate on this boy, he's my son." How is this possible?

Answer: Here are ten body parts with three letters: Arm, leg, eye, ear, toe, rib, jaw, gum, lip, and hip.

Answer: One of them is not a quarter, but the other one is. A dime and a quarter.

Answer: The surgeon is the boy's mother.

There are six purple socks, four red socks, and eight black socks all mixed up in a drawer. The socks are exactly the same except for the color. Your room is pitch black and you have to pick out one pair of matching socks. What is the least number of socks you would have to take out of the drawer to guarantee matching a pair?

Rita lives with her parents, on the fifteenth floor of an apartment building. Each morning she takes the elevator down to the lobby, where she waits for her schoolbus. After school the schoolbus drops her off at her building. She walks back through the lobby and enters the elevator, which she takes up to the sixth floor. At the sixth floor she gets out and walks up the remaining nine flights of stairs to get to her apartment. Why doesn't she take the elevator all the way up?

Answer: Four: It would be possible to get a matching pair in the first two that you pick out, but since you can't see, you'd have to take four to guarantee a match. If you pick out a purple sock, followed by a red one, then a black sock, then the next sock you pull out, whether it's purple, red, or black, will match one of the socks already in your hand.

Answer: Rita can't reach any buttons higher that the number six.

So...how do I look?

Here's much did the pirate pay for his earrings? *A buck an ear.* Who earns a living by driving customers away? *A cab driver.* When do dentists get angry? *When they run out of patients.* Our world is full of different types of people who, since the beginning of time, have had individual interests, various occupations, and distinctive fashion senses. The next pages explain how what we wear and what we do makes a statement about who we are.

Everyday People

Who? What? When? Wear?

People in different parts of the world have made clothing out of **tree bark**. The bark is stripped, packed down and pounded, then soaked in water and pounded some more until very soft. It is often painted before being elegantly draped around the body.

● ● ●

Did you know that the **tuxedo** was named after Lake Tuxedo in New York?

● ● ●

Back in ancient Rome, minor officials had narrow bands of red or purple edging their white togas, while very important people had broad bands of purple. The Emperor wore a toga that was all purple and embroidered with gold thread. Purple was the color of royalty because the dye was hard to make—from the murex, a type of shellfish that lived in the Mediterranean Sea—and therefore cost a lot.

● ● ●

Eighteenth-century **crinolines**—wide skirts with a hoop to hold the dress out like a lampshade—were very awkward, but one once saved a girl's life. She tried to commit suicide and jumped off a bridge. The crinoline acted like a parachute and she floated down to safety!

● ● ●

When giraffes were first introduced to the London Zoo in the 1830s, it set off a craze for dappled cloth!

● ● ●

The slide fastener—what we now call a **zipper**—was invented as a waterproof closure for rainboots in 1893, 35 years before the idea was adapted for use in clothing.

● ● ●

When **miniskirts** came out in the early 1960s, they were just above the knee; by the late 1960s they were so short, they almost weren't there.

● ● ●

Flared jeans are the one of the hottest trends, aren't they? Actually no. Fashioned on naval uniforms, flares, and the more extreme bell-bottoms, were made popular by singers and musicians in the 1960s.

Get Along, Little Doggie
Cowboys wore bandanas over their mouths to keep the dust out when they were herding cattle. Now they are a fashion statement—even for dogs!

Until the 20th century, fashionable swimming suits for women covered them from head to toe...or at least from neck to knee! In England and France in the 1700s, women were not to be seen "undressed" in their ankle-length, long-sleeved bathing dresses, so they changed in huts, which were wheeled down to the water—so they could delicately slip in for a swim unseen!

Hair Wear

Head hair is very important whichever culture you belong to. In some societies, people believe that hair has **special powers**. In the Bible, Samson was stronger than all the men in the land because he had long hair. His enemies had his hair cut off, and Samson lost his strength.

• • •

In Africa, **Masai** girls have shaved heads and the boys wear short hair.

• • •

French queen **Marie Antoinette** in the late 1700s wore her hair in such an elaborate pile that it made her look more than a head taller. She had her head cut off in the French Revolution—but not because of her hairstyle!

• • •

In southwestern United States, girls of the **Hopi** native people wore their hair in two big curls at the side of their head. These curls were called squash-blossom whorls, and showed the girls were available to be married.

• • •

Muslim men of the Sikh faith never cut their hair and keep it covered with a turban.

• • •

Up until the middle of the 20th century, calling something "**long hair**" meant that it was old-fashioned and boring. Then, in the 1960s, millions of young people all over the world started to wear their hair really long, and long hair was suddenly very hip!

WIGGING OUT!

Once upon a time in England, you could tell a man's profession by the shape of the **wig** he wore. Doctors, lawyers, and military officers all wore different kinds of wigs. Even today, British lawyers and judges wear special wigs.

• • •

In the 18th century, men and women wore very tall, white-powdered wigs called **Macaronis**. The bigger the wig, the more rich and important the person.

Hair to "Dye" For

If you wanted fashionable black hair about 400 years ago, you would use a lead comb. Unfortunately, because the comb could cause lead poisoning, you could literally become a fashion victim.

Where did the butcher go dancing?
At the meatball.

Which nail does a carpenter hate to hit?
His thumbnail.

Who is the strongest man in the world?
A policeman, because he can hold up as many cars as he wants with one hand.

Why did the girl take a ruler to bed?
She wanted to know how long she'd slept.

What did one geologist say to the other?
Let's go to the rock concert!

Why did the bank customer stand next to the bank vault?
He wanted to be on the safe side.

What did the bald man say when he got a comb for his birthday?
Thank you, I'll never part with it.

What was the newspaper headline when the escaped prisoners fell into cement?
Police arrest hardened criminals.

What would you get if you dropped a piano on an army officer?
A flat major.

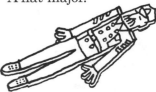

What's the name of the world's most famous under-water spy?
James Pond.

How many magicians does it take to change a light bulb?
Only one, but she changes it into a rabbit.

The Universal Smile

There are thousands of languages spoken and millions of different customs all over the world. But there is at least one thing that all humans understand: the smile. It means the same thing no matter who you are or where you live. Even babies who are blind from birth smile, so it must be a part of human behavior that we know without even having to learn it.

What do people in clock factories do all day?
They make faces.

Who earns a living by driving customers away?
A cab driver.

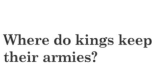

Why did the hairdresser win the race?
She took a shortcut.

How much did the pirate pay for his earrings?
A buck an ear.

Where do kings keep their armies?
Up their sleevies.

Hat's Off...to the Hat

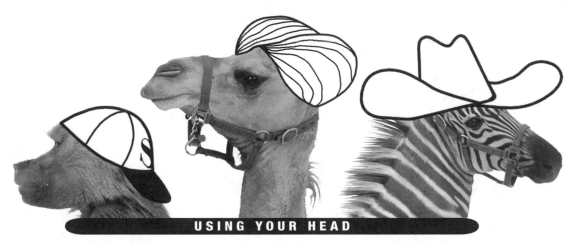

USING YOUR HEAD

Hats are a fashion statement in just about every part of the world.
And they're practical as well.

Wearing a **baseball cap** indoors and out has become a fashion statement. But wearing the visor anywhere but over your forehead means it can't work as it was designed—to keep the sun out of our eyes.

● ● ●

Nomadic people of the Sahara desert wear **turbans** wrapped around the head, face, and neck, leaving only the eyes exposed. The sun and sandstorms can be unbearable and this helps to protect them.

● ● ●

How about a hat that keeps the sun off your head and the rain from going down your neck—that can also be used as a water bowl? That's why the deluxe size of the classic cowboy hat, the **Stetson**, is called a ten-gallon hat!

Top-Secret Military Info

Centuries ago, soldiers who wore soft caps had iron skullcaps underneath for protection. Since these skullcaps were known as "secrets," telling someone to "keep it under your hat" means we want them to keep a secret.

A HEAD FOR DETAILS

When you watch a cowboy movie, you can tell the good guys from the bad guys by the color of their hats. What else can you tell about people by the hats they wear?

The **tam-o-shanter** from Scotland is a cap with a pompom on top. The different colors and tartan patterns help identify which clan the wearer belongs to.

• • •

The city of Venice, in Italy, is famous for its gondoliers, who will steer you down narrow canals in their boats, called gondolas. Just as famous are their straw hats. A **gondolier's hat** decorated with a red ribbon shows the wearer has at least five years experience at the job.

• • •

Everyone recognizes a chef's distinctive hat. **Chef's hats** used to—and sometimes still do—have 100 pleats. Why? Well, any famous chef would tell you that he was able to cook an egg a hundred different ways to please his master with a new dish every day. If you were that good you could wear a hat with 100 pleats. Nowadays disposable paper chef's hats are widely used, and they have only 48 pleats.

What is this?

Answer:
A snake that
swallowed a rhinoceros.

"A Swell Affair"

To Brush or Not to Brush

Nylon toothbrushes, like the one you use every day, weren't invented until 1938. That doesn't mean that people only started brushing their teeth then. Toothbrushes were actually invented around the late 1400s in China and were made out of animal hair, such as pig bristles.

When do dentists get angry?
When they run out of patients.

What do the two of us have in common?

We both have "the" same middle name.

Alexander the Great   Bozo the Clown

Why did the farmer drive a steamroller over her potato field?
So she could grow squash instead.

What does a farmer grow if he works very hard?
Tired.

Why did the nurse tiptoe past the medicine cabinet?
He didn't want to wake the sleeping pills.

What did the electrician say when she looked at the fuse box?
Nothing, she was too shocked.

Why did the scientist invent a better lightbulb?
She had a bright idea.

Why did the scientist put a knocker on his door?
He wanted to win the no bell prize.

Why did the tap dancer retire?
She kept falling into the sink.

Why do candle-makers only work two days a week?
They only work on wick-ends.

Why did the man put a clock under his desk?
He wanted to work over time.

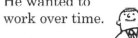

Why did the robber take a shower?
He wanted to make a clean getaway.

A butcher is six feet tall. What does he weigh?
Meat.

Why did the sailor drop to the floor?
The captain called "All hands on deck."

What did the boy say once he had learned how to count money? It all makes cents now.

Why did the girl put her money in the freezer? She wanted cold hard cash.

If a dollar and a nickel were at the top of a tall building, which would jump first? The nickel, it has less cents.

What's the best way to double your money? Fold it.

Why did the moon go to the bank? To get its first quarter.

When does it rain money? When there's change in the weather.

What's a doughnut? Someone who's crazy about money.

What has a head and tail but no body?

A quarter.

Big Pengoes

In Hungary in 1946 a bank note was issued for 100 quintillion pengoes, which looks like this: 100,000,000,000,000,000,000.

What did the violin say to the musician?

Stop picking on me.

Which band member is most likely to be struck by lightning?
The conductor.

Why did the DJ put an old shoe in his ear?
He liked to listen to sole music.

What kind of music does your father like to sing?
Pop music.

Did you hear the one about the musician who wrote all his music in bed?
He insisted on writing sheet music.

Which composer runs around castles?
Moat-zart.

How does the sky listen to music?
Through the cloud-speaker.

How do you make a bandstand?
Take their chairs away.

What keeps jazz musicians on Earth?
Groovity.

Making Music

Did you know that Beethoven, who composed some of the world's best-loved music, was deaf? He used to cut the legs off his pianos so he could "hear" what he was playing by feeling the vibrations the music made through the floor.

91

Why would you take a pencil to bed?
To draw the curtains.

Did you hear the story about the pencil?
Oh, forget it, there's no point.

What has teeth but can't eat?
A comb.

What did the scissors say to the hair?
It won't be long now.

What do you call a snowman with a suntan?
A puddle.

What did one firecracker say to the other?
My pop is bigger than your pop.

What has wheels and flies?
A garbage truck.

If two's company and three's a crowd, what's four and five?
Nine.

What kind of saw dances?
A jigsaw.

Try Saying This Three Times Fast!

Pneumonoultramicroscopicsilicovolcanoconiosis.
It's almost impossible to pronounce this word, let alone guess its meaning. Apart from the fact that it's a medical disease, it's also the longest word (all 45 letters of it!) in the Oxford English Dictionary.

What do you know about nitrates?
They're cheaper than day rates.

What did the limestone say to the geologist?
Don't take me for granite.

Who steals the soap in the bathroom?

The robber ducky.

Why would snow and rain make a good bed?
Snow comes in blankets and rain in sheets.

How many sides does a shoebox have?
Two—the inside and the outside.

What kind of ship never sinks?
A friendship.

What goes through a door but never comes in or out?
A keyhole.

What's the difference between a newspaper and a TV?
Try swatting a fly with a TV and you'll find out.

What did the shovel say to the pile of earth?
I dig you.

Face Facts

Just about every culture has used masks, not just as a form of fashion, but in religious festivals and carnivals too.

Today we wear masks at **Halloween**, for masquerade parties, and for Carnival parades and celebrations—for the fun of it!

• • •

In Puerto Rico, painted masks are made from hollowed out **calabash**, which is a sort of gourd.

• • •

In Papua New Guinea, ceremonial masks are made from mud and clay and are decorated with local berries.

• • •

Lots of cultures have used masks to dress up their **dead** before they bury them. One of the most famous is the gold mask of young King Tutankhamen. The cobra and vulture on the forehead of the mask show that he was ruler of Egypt.

KISS AND MAKEUP

Looking good in ancient Rome wasn't easy. Facial masks made from sheep fat and breadcrumbs soaked in milk were left to sit for a while before using—the smell was probably revolting. Women used face makeup made of very toxic substances, such as white lead. Men shaved with iron razors and no soap—ow! On their nicks and cuts, they would plaster "band-aids" made of spider webs soaked in oil and vinegar.

• • •

For centuries in Europe washing yourself was unpopular. Heavy makeup and beauty patches were used to cover up skin blemishes and diseases.

He or She?
Both men and women wore makeup in 17th-century Europe.

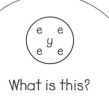

What is this?

Answer:
Crossed eyes

Highwire Acts

The first circuses, in the late eighteenth century, were shows of trick equestrianism involving amazing feats with horses and their riders. In the late nineteenth century, new acts were introduced to the circus. Still a favorite today, the flying trapeze was invented by a French gymnast at this time. His name might sound familiar. Jules Léotard gave his name to the stretchy one-piece garment still worn by many circus artists and dancers today.

Deep in Your Sole

Winkle Pickers were what the British called shoes with very pointed toes—pointy enough to dig a snail (or winkle) out of its shell. Of course if you wore them, your toes got very squished, and you had to put up with sore feet and corns on your toes! Ugh.

High-Class Shoes
In Europe in the 1800s, a woman had to be an aristocrat to wear fancy shoes. They were made of velvet and buttoned up the side—and always matched her dress.

Got to know your right shoe from your left, right? Not in the 16th and 17th centuries, when soldiers' boots were made to fit on either foot. It was probably uncomfortable, but switching boots between feet let them last longer, or at least wear out at the same time.

• • •

Japanese sandals, called **geta**, have thongs that fit between the big toe and one beside it. **Tabi** are special socks that look like mittens—with a separate section for the big toe—made especially to wear with them.

• • •

Fashion reached new heights when **high heels** were invented in the 17th century—for men! Short men sometimes wore heels up to 12 cm (5 inches) to boost their egos.

• • •

The French word for a wooden shoe is "sabot." When some French workers lost their jobs to machines, they threw their wooden shoes into the machines to wreck them. That's where we get the word "**sabotage**."

• • •

In 1958, a long-distance runner was unhappy with the sneakers he wore for running. With his coach, he formed a company to design athletic shoes, and named it after the Greek goddess of victory—**Nike**.

Click Your Heels Together...
When Judy Garland starred as Dorothy in the movie *The Wizard of Oz*, eight pairs of ruby slippers were made for her. In the year 2000, the last pair was auctioned—and sold for $665,000.

What type of sandals do frogs wear?

Open toad!

What's a boxer's favorite drink?
Punch.

What kind of socks do baseball players wear?
Ones with runs in them.

Why are basketball players sloppy eaters?
They're always dribbling.

Which football player wears the biggest shoes?
The one with the biggest feet.

Size 18

Why does it get hot after a baseball game?
All the fans have left.

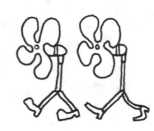

Why did the football coach go to the bank?
He wanted to get his quarter back.

Why is tennis such a noisy game?
Each player raises a racket.

Why is a baseball team similar to a cake?
They both depend on their batters.

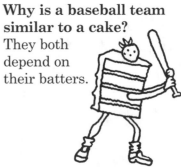

Why do basketball players have long arms?
If their arms were any shorter they wouldn't reach their hands.

What can be served but not eaten?
A tennis ball.

What is a football player's favorite drink?

Penal tea.

How are tennis players like judges?
They spend a lot of time at the court.

Why do soccer players do so well in math?
They know how to use their heads.

How do hockey players greet each other?
By "hi" sticking.

What letter does golf start with?
A tee.

Take Heart

In an average week, assuming you exercise, your heart will beat about 1 million times. When it's very active, your heart can pump about 75 liters (20 gallons) of blood each minute. That's enough to fill a bathtub every 2 minutes!

School Daze

How Does Your Eraser Erase?

A pencil is made of graphite. When you write on paper, tiny particles of gritty graphite are left on the paper and in the paper fiber. When you rub your eraser across the paper, the rubber picks up the bits of graphite, and like magic, your pencil marks disappear!

A blackboard.

What is white when it's dirty and black when it's clean?

Why did Bennie take a ladder to school?

He wanted to go to high school.

How do you make sure you pass a geometry test?

Know all the angles.

My teacher got mad at me for something I didn't do.

What was that?

My homework!

Why did the Cyclops give up teaching?

He only had one pupil.

Why did the student return her math book?

It had too many problems.

Why did the teacher wear sunglasses in class?

Because her students were so bright.

Laugh Attack

Laughs come in all sizes. Whether it's a loud guffaw or an uncontrollable fit of the giggles, laughter has incredible physical effects on our bodies. What exactly happens when you laugh? Around fifteen of your facial muscles contract. When you laugh really hard, you might become weak at the knees, get a stomachache, even shed some tears. Your respiratory system also moves into action. Your windpipe half-closes and you take in air irregularly. Meanwhile, chemical blood sensors tell your body it's running out of air. In response, your heart pumps faster, sending more blood to your muscles. Phew! Sounds like a total body workout!

Laughter on the Brain

Believe it or not, there is such a thing! Gelotology is the scientific name for the study of laughter. Scientists know that parts of our brains are responsible for specific bodily functions. For instance, our frontal lobes are responsible for our emotions. But since we laugh for many different reasons, there's more than one spot on our brains that allows us to do this.

Laugh Facts

Surprise!

If you've ever tried tickling yourself, you know it's impossible. Why? Your brain needs to be tense and surprised for tickling to work. When you try to do it to yourself, your brain is in control and you know exactly where you are going to be tickled and what it will feel like. When someone else tickles you, it's a different story. You even react to the thought of being tickled. Your nerves become sensitive in the same way they do when you are excited or afraid.

Funny Funny Bone

The funny thing about your funny bone is that it's not a bone at all. What you're really hitting is your ulnar nerve, the nerve that carries messages to and from your brain and fingers. Most of your nerves are well protected by skin and flesh. But for some reason—and scientists are not sure why—your ulnar nerve doesn't have much padding where it passes through your elbow. So when you bump your elbow, you often hit the nerve, sending a weird tingly feeling to your fingers.

Surely You Jest

What people think is funny has changed a lot over time, but one thing's for sure: comedy itself has been around a long, long time. The first stand-up comedians came on the scene about 4,500 years ago to entertain the Egyptian Pharaohs. English and French kings, around 500-1,000 years ago, kept court comedians, called "fools" or "jesters." They were often treated poorly. They were usually dwarves, often deformed people, who were paid to dress up and entertain at banquets with their pranks and amusing chatter. Although these jesters were thought to not be very intelligent people, in fact their position often allowed them to make outrageous and rude comments to kings, queens, and Pharaohs that other "servants" wouldn't dare.

Laughter... Pass It On

Sometimes you don't even have to know what's funny to enjoy the benefits of a good laugh. Have you ever been around friends and someone starts laughing, then another person, and even though you don't know what they are laughing about you start laughing too? Sometimes it can take ages to stop. Even if you never find out what started the giggle session, you'll feel great after.

More Laugh Facts

☹ Sad to Glad ☺

Usually we laugh because something's funny, but laughter is also a tension-release mechanism to help us feel better if we're in an uncomfortable situation. Say your teacher asks you a question in front of the whole class and you draw a complete blank. You might laugh when you don't know the answer, but not because you really think it's funny. In fact, you may feel pretty embarrassed. But laughing helps you get rid of some of your tension. Laughing sensors in your body send signals to your brain, activating neurons that tell you that you feel good.

You Think That's Funny?

Imagine this: your baby brother comes into your room and knocks over a model you've been working on. Because of his age and lack of experience he may find it very funny that bits and pieces of your work go flying all over the room. He's just not old enough to understand. Or, you might hear an adult roar with laughter about something that you don't find at all funny. Things like which country we come from, how we are raised, and our ages all contribute to what we find funny.

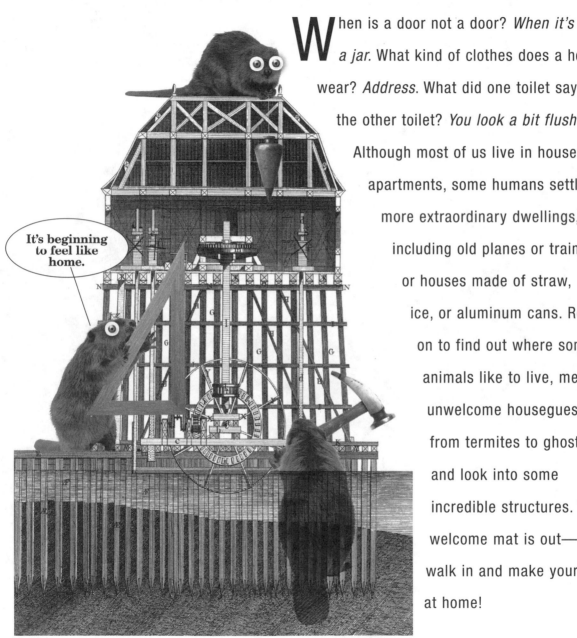

It's beginning to feel like home.

When is a door not a door? *When it's a jar.* What kind of clothes does a house wear? *Address.* What did one toilet say to the other toilet? *You look a bit flushed.* Although most of us live in houses or apartments, some humans settle in more extraordinary dwellings, including old planes or trains, or houses made of straw, ice, or aluminum cans. Read on to find out where some animals like to live, meet unwelcome houseguests from termites to ghosts, and look into some incredible structures. The welcome mat is out— walk in and make yourself at home!

108

House and Home

Home, Sweet Home

LITTLE PIG, LET ME IN...

Remember the story of the Three Little Pigs, and their houses of straw, wood, and brick?

Straw houses exist, and not just in storybooks. Slabs of compressed straw are covered with cement plaster to create well-insulated walls. In Australia, straw houses built 60 years ago are still being lived in today.

• • •

Along the southern coast of Papua New Guinea, the Motuan people have houses built on **wooden stilts** over the sea. These stilt houses can last up to about 30 years, depending on the type of wood used for the posts that hold the house up.

PIG NUMBER THREE

Brick homes can stand up to the Big Bad Wolf— and last hundreds of years.

Mud houses, or **adobes**, are a popular choice of home in the southwestern United States. The bricks of clay, sand, and water are extremely hard and make excellent walls. Many early adobe homes date back 1,000 years.

• • •

Shibam, a city in Yemen, has mud-brick houses up to 12 floors tall and hundreds of years old.

• • •

There are still buildings standing that the **Aztec** people of Central America built hundreds of years ago. They mixed animal blood into the mortar they used to hold the bricks together.

PIG OF THE FUTURE

The **Earthship** homes some people have built are more or less indestructible as well as being environmentally friendly. The main parts of the building are made of recycled car tires filled with compacted earth, which are like big bricks covered in steel-belted rubber.

Add a Dash of Ash

It's only recently that people found out the secret ingredient the ancient Romans put in their concrete—concrete used to build structures that have lasted more than 2,000 years. It's a kind of ash thrown out by Vesuvius and similar volcanoes.

No Return for Deposit

A man in Houston, Texas, has used 39,000 flattened beer cans as aluminum siding to decorate his house. He also uses the cans to make wind chimes, drapes, and streamers.

Knock knock.
Who's there?
Lettuce.
Lettuce who?
**Lettuce in,
it's cold outside!**

112

Have an Ice Day

There's nothing like reaching into your refrigerator on a hot day to take out a cool drink. And think of all the food in there that would go bad if it were left out. But what did people do before there were fridges to keep food cold and fresh? Imagine walking up to the top of a mountain to lug snow and ice home to use as your refrigerator. That's what the ancient Greeks and Romans did. They dug holes in the ground, lined them with logs and straw, packed in snow and ice, and covered them up. Believe it or not, the ice and snow compressed and stayed frozen for months.

Amazing Structures

All over the world, ancient people managed to take massive stones and set them up on end. These stones are called **megaliths**—*mega* means big, *liths* means stones. Near the famous **Stonehenge** in England, the Avebury Rings are three circles that were at one time made up of around 98 huge stones. The site is so big that there is a whole village inside it.

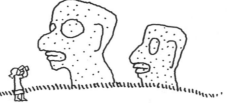

Easter Island (also called Isla de Pascua in Spanish, or Rapanui in Polynesian) lies in the remote southeastern Pacific Ocean. Carved from solid rock hundreds—possibly thousands—of years ago, huge stone statues of men's heads were placed at the edge of the island, facing inward rather than towards the sea. Were they built for the gods, or as protection for the island? We may never know.

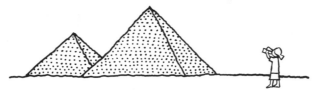

Can you imagine a building containing 2.3 million blocks of stone, each one weighing as much as a tour bus? The building, one of the Seven Wonders of the World, is the **Pyramid of Khufu**, also called the Great Pyramid of Egypt. Archeologists are still speculating as to how the workers who built the pyramid moved the blocks of stone higher and higher up. Did thousands of men use pulleys and ropes, or did they construct machinery that we don't know about? What do you think?

The **West Edmonton Mall** in Alberta, Canada, is one of the largest shopping and entertainment complexes in the world, spanning the equivalent of 48 city blocks. It's got 58 entrances, a huge indoor lake, an amusement park, bungy jumping, a hotel with 354 rooms, 325,000 light fixtures, 110 restaurants, 21 movie theaters and a parking lot the size of more than 104 football fields.

The **Tsing Ma Bridge** in Hong Kong is 2.2 km (1.4 miles) long, making it the world's longest span suspension bridge.

As crazy as it may seem, the timekeeping of the famous **Big Ben** clock in London, England, is regulated by a pile of coins, stacked on the pendulum!

Did you know that the **Great Wall of China** is the only structure made by humans large enough to be seen from space? It is 2,575 km (1,600 miles) long, and after 2,000 years is still standing.

Said to be the most beautiful building in the world, the **Taj Mahal** in India took 22 years to build and employed over 20,000 workers.

Knock knock.
Who's there?
Alexia.
Alexia who?
Alexia again to open this door!

Knock! Knock!
Who's there?
Police.
Police who?
**Police open the door,
it's freezing out here.**

Knock! Knock!
Who's there?
MT.
MT who?
**MT your glass before
you take more.**

Knock! Knock!
Who's there?
Tank.
Tank who?
You're welcome!

Knock! Knock!
Who's there?
Dish.
Dish who?
Dish is a very bad joke.

Knock! Knock!
Who's there?
Butcher.
Butcher who?
**Butcher can't touch
your toes.**

Knock! Knock!
Who's there?
Time.
Time who?
**Time you got yourself
a watch.**

Knock! Knock!
Who's there?
Waiter.
Waiter who?
**Waiter minute, I'm
almost ready.**

Knock! Knock!
Who's there?
Beets.
Beets who?
Beets me!

Knock! Knock!
Who's there?
Doughnut.
Doughnut who?
**Doughnut open your
door for strangers.**

Knock! Knock!
Who's there?
Alaska.
Alaska who?
Alaska only once.

Knock! Knock!
Who's there?
Ya.
Ya who?
I didn't know you were in the rodeo.

Knock! Knock!
Who's there?
Carl.
Carl who?
Carl me back when you've got time to talk.

Knock! Knock!
Who's there?
Wooden.
Wooden who?
Wooden you like to know.

Knock! Knock!
Who's there?
Icon.
Icon who?
Icon tell another Knock! Knock! joke if you want.

Knock! Knock!
Who's there?
House.
House who?
House it going?

Knock! Knock!
Who's there?
Acme.
Acme who?
Acme another question.

Knock! Knock!
Who's there?
Anita.
Anita who?
Anita lot more to eat, I'm starving.

Knock! Knock!
Who's there?
Hammy.
Hammy who?
Hammy a wrench so I can fix this thing.

Homes on the Move

Would you enjoy living in an **airplane** for life? One company is taking disused Boeing 727s and converting them to private residences. They are cemented to large blocks, and guaranteed not to fly!

If you don't like the idea of a plane, you can always live in a **train car** that has been converted into a home. It can be moved to just about anywhere you want. In England, disused trains are being remodeled and used as restaurants.

All over the world people live on **yachts** that sail the ocean, or **barges** and **houseboats** that go along canal routes and lakes. Or how about a stationary houseboat moored alongside other houseboats?

We All Live in a Russian Submarine

Unless you're in the Russian Navy, you wouldn't be living in one, but…a Typhoon submarine is the world's biggest, almost three times as long as a Boeing 747 airplane!

118

Book a room at **Jules Undersea Lodge**, the world's only underwater hotel, and dive right in (literally!). The lodge is 6 1/2 m (21 ft) deep in a natural mangrove lagoon in Key Largo, Florida.

Want to have a *really* cool vacation? Try the **Ice Hotel** in Quebec. Every year, in about five days, a new hotel is built out of 12,193,000 kg (12,000 tons) of snow and 406,500 kg (400 tons) of ice. There is a similar hotel in Sweden.

For a really expensive vacation, you could stay at the **Burj Al Arab**, the Arabian Tower hotel in Dubai, United Arab Emirates. It is the world's tallest hotel, with 27 double-height stories. Hungry? Just take an elevator up to the scenic restaurant suspended high above the sea, or down to the underwater restaurant.

Can you guess what this drawing is?

Answer:
A man with his bowtie caught in an elevator door.

Knock! Knock!
Who's there?
A door.
A door who?
**Adorable me,
that's who!**

Knock! Knock!
Who's there?
You.
You who?
Are you calling me?

Knock! Knock!
Who's there?
Weed.
Weed who?
**Weed better do the dishes
before Mom gets home.**

Knock! Knock!
Who's there?
Butcher.
Butcher who?
**Butcher didn't think
you'd see me again.**

Knock! Knock!
Who's there?
Watch.
Watch who?
**Watch you want to do
for lunch?**

Knock! Knock!
Who's there?
Little old lady.
Little old lady who?
**I didn't know you could
yodel.**

Knock! Knock!
Who's there?
Isabel.
Isabel who?
**Isabel working or do I
have to knock?**

Knock! Knock!
Who's there?
Turnip.
Turnip who?
**Turnip on time, or you'll
miss the surprise.**

Knock! Knock!
Who's there?
Ice cream.
Ice cream who?
**Ice cream, you scream,
we all scream for ice
cream.**

Knock! Knock!
Who's there?
Must.
Must who?
Must you keep saying that?

Knock! Knock!
Who's there?
Oscar.
Oscar who?
Oscar if she can come out to play.

Knock! Knock!
Who's there?
Aardvark.
Aardvark who?
Aardvark a million miles for one of your smiles.

Knock! Knock!
Who's there?
Francis.
Francis who?
Francis my favorite country in Europe.

Knock! Knock!
Who's there?
Ivana.
Ivana who?
Ivana suck your blood!

Knock! Knock!
Who's there?
Banana.
Banana who?
Knock! Knock!
Who's there?
Banana.
Banana who?
Knock! Knock!
Who's there?
Banana.
Banana who?
Knock! Knock!
Who's there?
Orange.
Orange who?
Orange you glad I didn't say banana?

Knock! Knock!
Who's there?
Henrietta.
Henrietta who?
Henrietta large pizza and didn't share with anyone.

Knock! Knock!
Who's there?
Ima.
Ima who?
Ima tired of knocking, can't you just open the door?

Haunted Houses

SELL THE FARM

A house in England was said to be haunted by a farmer who had lived and died there a long time ago. A family living in the house reported that the radio would come on full blast in the middle of the night, tuned to a foreign-language station. Lampshades flew across the room. One year the Christmas tree started rocking violently for no reason. On New Year's Eve they heard a knocking at the door. They answered it to find a very angry man in old-fashioned clothing threatening them about living there. After four years of this, the family sold the house and moved. The new owners have never reported hearing or seeing anything unusual.

In the Army for Life...and Beyond

In Niagara Falls at Fort George, the ghosts of Canadian, British, and American soldiers have been seen wandering around the fort.

Where would you go to find ghosts? Some spots seem to make better ghost homes than others, including ancient places, cemeteries, churches, and places where people have died.

York, one of the oldest towns in England, was founded as a fort by the Romans around 71 A.D. People claim to have seen ghosts all over town, including in the Minster, the church that has survived from medieval times. York still has cobblestone streets, but they are on higher ground than they used to be back in Roman times. So, when people see ghosts of Roman soldiers in York, the phantom marchers are **knee-deep** in the ground!

The Los Angeles **Pet Cemetery** in California is a graveyard where pets of the rich and famous are buried. People say they have seen animal ghosts come back from their final resting places there to play. Perhaps the most famous is the spirit of the Great Dane Kabar, a dog that belonged to silent-movie star Rudolph Valentino. Kabar, who died in 1929, is reportedly seen near its grave, and licks people who pass by.

Knock! Knock!
Who's there?
Boo.
Boo who?
Don't cry, it's only a joke.

123

Knock! Knock!
Who's there?
Comb.
Comb who?
Comb over and see my new puppy.

Knock! Knock!
Who's there?
Bean.
Bean who?
Bean anywhere nice lately?

Knock! Knock!
Who's there?
Penny.
Penny who?
Penny for your thoughts.

Knock! Knock!
Who's there?
Peek.
Peek who?
Peek-a-boo.

Knock! Knock!
Who's there?
Jigsaw.
Jigsaw who?
Jigsaw you peeping through the window.

Knock! Knock!
Who's there?
Jess.
Jess who?
Jess me and my shadow.

Knock! Knock!
Who's there?
Yolanda.
Yolanda who?
Yolanda me some money?

Knock! Knock!
Who's there?
Kent.
Kent who?
Kent you tell by my voice?

Knock! Knock!
Who's there?
Hans.
Hans who?
Hans off the TV remote control, I'm watching this show.

Knock! Knock!
Who's there?
Ben.
Ben who?
Ben knocking on your door all afternoon!

Knock! Knock!
Who's there?
Hutch.
Hutch who?
Bless you!

Knock! Knock!
Who's there?
Eileen.
Eileen who?
Eileen over to tie my shoe!

Knock! Knock!
Who's there?
Olive.
Olive who?
Olive you! How do you feel about me?

Knock! Knock!
Who's there?
Justin.
Justin who?
Justin case you were wondering.

Knock! Knock!
Who's there?
Justin.
Justin who?
Justin time for dinner!

Knock! Knock!
Who's there?
Les.
Les who?
Les go for a swim!

Knock! Knock!
Who's there?
Sarah.
Sarah who?
Sarah doctor in the house?

Knock! Knock!
Who's there?
Nobody.
If nobody's there, then who's telling the joke?

Animal Homes

Insects build some of the world's most impressive structures. **Termites** build mud mounds up to 3 m (10 ft) tall. That's like people building a castle more than eight stories tall out of mud, using buckets and spades and spit!

● ● ●

Beavers don't just build homes but lodges. They chew down trees to dam a stream, so that the water level rises to hide the lodge entrance. The lodge includes a sleeping platform built above the water level, and an area for collecting and storing food, so the **beavers** stay snug and safe through the cold northern winter.

● ● ●

Romantic birds? The male **bowerbird** of Australia builds an elaborate structure on the ground to attract a mate. He neatly locks together twigs and sticks. Then he decorates the inside with flowers, parrot feathers, berries and—when he can find them—shiny bits of tin foil, glass, or beads.

● ● ●

The **false scorpion** builds a nest shaped like an igloo—but only about as big as a thimble! And good thing it's made from sand, because a real igloo would certainly melt in the hot areas of North America, Europe, and Africa where the false scorpion lives. It glues together sand grains and bits of wood and stone with fine silk threads for its nest, being careful to leave a tiny hole open so it can collect more building material. Not until it is satisfied and the hole is sealed will the false scorpion start laying its eggs.

● ● ●

Most animals build their own homes, but not all. The **hermit crab** likes living in the homes of other creatures. Since they don't have hard shells to protect their soft bodies, hermit crabs find empty shells and move in.

● ● ●

Siamese fighting fish hatch their eggs in nests made of bubbles. The male fish gulps air through his mouth and shoots the bubbles out through his gills. Covered with sticky mucus, the bubbles float upwards, where they remain held together in the leaves of water plants.

A lot of people think of **bears** living in dens inside caves. In fact, some bears make nest homes out of branches and fallen leaves. Some live in hollow trees, even hollowing out their own dens at the bases of trees.

127

Knock! Knock!
Who's there?
A little kid.
A little kid who?
A little kid who can't reach the doorbell!

Will you remember me in 10 years?
Yes.
Will you remember me next year?
Yes.
Will you remember me next month?
Yes.
Will you remember me next week?
Yes.
Will you remember me in a minute?
Yes.
Knock! Knock!
Who's there?
I thought you said you'd remember me.

Knock! Knock!
Who's there?
Abbot.
Abbot who?
Abbot you don't know who this is.

Knock! Knock!
Who's there?
Radio.
Radio who?
Radio not, here I come.

Knock! Knock!
Who's there?
Alison.
Alison who?
Alison to music every night when I'm falling asleep.

Knock! Knock!
Who's there?
Adore.
Adore who?
Adore is between us, open up!

Knock! Knock!
Who's there?
Dwayne.
Dwayne who?
Dwayne the bathtub, I'm dwowning!

Knock! Knock!
Who's there?
Zombies.
Zombies who?
Zombies make honey, zombies just buzz around.

Knock! Knock!
Who's there?
Canoe.
Canoe who?
Canoe open the door?

Knock! Knock!
Who's there?
Cow.
Cow who?
Cow are you doing?

Knock! Knock!
Who's there?
Alex.
Alex who?
Alex plain later, just let me in.

Knock! Knock!
Who's there?
Barry.
Barry who?
Barry nice to meet you.

Knock! Knock!
Who's there?
Russian.
Russian who?
Russian around all day to get here on time.

Knock! Knock!
Who's there?
Howard!
Howard who?
Howard you like to go and get an ice cream?

Knock! Knock!
Who's there?
Noah.
Noah who?
Noah more jokes!

Knock! Knock!
Go away!

Knock! Knock!
Who's there?
Ima.
Ima who?
Ima not lying. That was it. There aren't any more jokes. Please stop knocking.

Unwelcome House Guests

BUGS WITH BITE

Most of us aren't sharing our beds with **bed bugs**. And that's a good thing, as they do like feeding on humans—especially on human blood.

If the bed bug isn't bad enough, how about human **lice**? These tiny insects love to make their homes in human hair on just about every part of your body.

If you have a dog or cat, **fleas** can make them itch like crazy. Even with all the anti-flea products on the market, it can take 30 days or more to get rid of a flea infestation in your house, as fleas like to hide in carpets and floorboards.

"COME INTO MY PARLOR," SAID THE SPIDER

Of the more than 2,500 kinds of spiders in North America, a few are **house spiders**. Spiders love living in crevices or little tunnels they make for themselves in basements—and just about everywhere. The timid spider makes a good house guest, trapping other insects you might not want to have lurking around.

Dining on the Table

If you don't have termites, there might just be woodworm eating through your furniture!

EATING YOU OUT OF HOUSE AND HOME

No home wants **termites**! Termites will quietly eat all the wood in your house if you don't stop them. They build little mud shelter tubes along foundation walls and ceilings, connecting to their colony. Worker termites use the tunnels to carry food—meals of wood—back and forth along the tunnels.

HOME INVASION

Like most other insects, **cockroaches** multiply like crazy and can soon completely take over your home. Just one can have about 30 offspring per month. And if that's not enough to have you looking for a bigger place to live, some female cockroaches can produce young without even mating, in a process called parthenogenesis.

What did the police officer say when a spider ran down her back?

You're under a vest!

Why are fish so smart? *Because they live in schools.* What lies at the bottom of the sea and shakes? *A nervous wreck.* What do you get when you graduate from scuba-diving school? *A deep-loma.* From the deepest oceans to freshwater ponds, our Earth is made up of nearly three quarters water, so it makes sense that lake monsters, giant squids, sharks, sailors, and fishy families fascinate us. Find out the shocking truth about electric eels, put on your swim fins, plug your nose, and dive into the exciting pages ahead.

Water World

Getting in the Swim of Things

THE LONG SWIM HOME

Some fish travel amazingly long distances. The **Pacific salmon** is born in fresh water and travels down to the ocean to grow. Once it is grown up, it travels all the way back up the stream to where it was born, battling its way up rushing rivers. It swims up into the shallows and then lays its eggs and dies.

FISH FARTS?

Watch for the **bubbles** popping from the vent on a shark's belly! It's not being rude, only using air to help it float. A shark will swim to the surface, gulp air and swallow it into its stomach. Then it can release air to keep its position.

SHARK ATTACK

Every time a shark loses a **tooth**, it is replaced. A shark may grow 24,000 teeth in a lifetime.

● ● ●

As well as having extremely sensitive noses that can pick up the scent of blood from a long way off, sharks have pores on their heads that lead to special receptors able to detect the **electrical fields** given off by animals—including humans!

● ● ●

Sharks even **eat** each other. A tiger shark measuring 4 m (13 ft)—as long as a small car—was seen to grab a gray reef shark that was more than half its own size. It bit the gray reef shark in half, in less time than it took to blink! After the second bite all that was left were the pectoral fins and head.

SEAFOOD LEFTOVERS

When salmon die after laying eggs, nature's clean-up crew of scavengers—including bears, eagles, and seagulls—eat the dead fish along the river banks. The sea is full of scavenger fish:

Young marine **eels** eat dead fish and crustaceans.

● ● ●

Remoras swim near sharks and other large fish, eating their left-overs.

● ● ●

Sharks keep the ocean clean by eating dead or wounded fish.

Dolphins need to breathe air, because they are mammals. At night they lie just below the surface of the water and, even in their sleep, rise to the surface for air.

135

By the sea

What is a shrimp's favorite place to shop?
At a prawn-shop.

What did the crab buy at the bakery?
Chocolate e-claws.

Why are fishermen like mad dogs?
They always want a bite.

What's the best way to catch a fish?
Have someone throw it to you.

What part of the fish weighs the most?
The scales.

Why is the sea salty?
Because fish don't like pepper.

How does the sea greet the sand?
It waves.

What's the difference between the Earth and the sea?
The Earth is dirty, but the sea is tide-y.

Why does the ocean roar?
You would too if you had sharks in your bed!

Which is the best day to go to the beach?
Sun-day.

What can fall on the sea without getting wet?
Your shadow.

What kind of bed does a mermaid sleep in?
A water bed.

When is a boat not a boat?
When it's a-float.

What washes up on small beaches?
Micro-waves.

A Whale of a Size!

Blue whales are the largest animals in the world. An average male is as long as a basketball court—and the females are bigger. Even newborn blue whales weigh as much as a full-grown Indian elephant!

Home, Wet Home

People have claimed to see monsters living in lakes all over the world— and each monster has its own name:

For over a hundred years, people in Scotland have claimed that Loch (or Lake) Ness is the home of **Nessie**, the Loch Ness Monster. Despite underwater expeditions and thousands of people with cameras, we don't have any real proof that the world's most famous freshwater monster exists.

• • •

In Sweden, at Lake Gryttjen, another freshwater monster called **Gryttie** is being investigated. Some believe that Gryttie may be a lone manatee, a large, elusive mammal that lives underwater.

• • •

Living in Lake Champlain, where New York, Vermont, and Quebec meet, there is said to be a creature known as **Champ**. No one has seen Champ for about 300 years.

• • •

In Lake Okanagan in British Columbia, legend says there lives a monster with a wonderful name— **Ogopogo**!

THERE GOES THE NEIGHBORHOOD

The only place in the world you'll find a **devil's hole pupfish** is in a limestone cave in the Nevada desert, in a pool so deep that no one has located its bottom. These fish have existed for more than 12,000 years, since the time when the Nevada desert wasn't a desert at all. It used to be a wet area where an interesting population of water life lived, but almost all of the lakes and rivers dried up.

No One's Home
Sea water flows into the Dead Sea in the Middle East and evaporates, leaving so much salt that almost nothing can live there.

FISHY FAMILIES

The male **seahorse** has a pouch in which the female lays her eggs. It's the father that looks after the eggs for around two months until they hatch, and cares for the "seafoals" until they are ready to be on their own.

• • •

When a female **stickleback** fish is ready to lay her eggs, the male goes to work. He digs a hole in the mud, then builds a tube-shaped nest for the eggs, using weeds and bits of gravel glued together with mucus.

• • •

A father **sea catfish** doesn't eat for several weeks, while he keeps the eggs of his young in his mouth until they are ready to hatch.

• • •

Most fish mothers abandon their babies when they are still eggs, but not the **tilapia**. A tilapia mother looks after her young—if the babies are threatened she opens her mouth and lets the babies swim inside where it's safe.

Why are fish so smart?

They swim in schools.

Gone Fishing

krill
krill
krill

ALL-YOU-CAN-EAT SHRIMP SPECIAL

An adult humpback whale eats more than 1,000 kg (1 ton) of krill a day. What's **krill**? Tiny fish and shrimp.

• • •

The humpback whale feeds by taking a huge mouthful of water, closing its lips and then squeezing the water out again. On the way out, the water passes through feathery filters called **baleen** that strain out the krill. Simple.

• • •

The skin below the humpback's lower jaw is pleated, and unfolds as the whale takes a huge swallow. Scientists believe that a hungry humpback can hold more than 55,000 liters (15,000 gallons) of water—enough to fill more than 400 bathtubs—in its mouth at one time!

Fish Fishing for Fish

A football fish has a built-in fishing rod on the top of its head. The rod is a barb tipped with a glowing lure. Nosey little fishes soon find themselves on the football fish's menu.

TAKE AIM

The **archerfish** can shoot its lunch from a distance of 1.5 m (5 ft)—by spitting. It swims just under the surface of the water until it spies bugs or spiders on the grass and twigs hanging over the water. Then the fish fires droplets of water that hit the prey and knock it to the surface—where it gets gobbled up!

WHEN GOOD FISH GO BAD

Why does fish smell fishy? Fresh fish doesn't smell at all—really. Fish begins to smell when it starts to go bad. Once a fish dies, nitrogen compounds in its body start to decay and convert into carbon-based molecules called **amines**, which cause the smell we call "fishy."

Tongue Twister:
Fried fresh fish,
Fish fried fresh,
Fresh fried fish,
Fresh fish fried,
Or fish fresh fried.

Ocean Records

SMALLEST SWIMMERS

The smallest fish in the world is the *trimattum nanus* of the Chagus Archipelago in the Indian Ocean. It is less than 8.5 mm (⅓ inch) long—that's the size of a grain of rice.

The smallest **sea star** is only 1.83 cm (¾ inch) in diameter, smaller than a piece of popped popcorn.

SUPER-SIZED SQUID

An **Antarctic squid** can grow to be 20 m (65 ft) long, and some dead ones have been found even bigger than that. That's about the same length as five cars lined up bumper to bumper.

A stranded **giant squid** found on a New Zealand beach back in the 1800s was nearly 18 m (60 ft) from the tip of its mantle to the tips of its 12-m (40-ft) tentacles. It was estimated to weigh about 1,000 kg (1 ton), and its eyes were the size of a person's head!

Blue whale: 30 m (98 ft), estimated 81,000 kg (80 tons)—the size of about 900 full-grown men!

Whale of a Noise-Maker

A sperm whale has two pairs of lips beneath the blowhole on top of its head. They clap together when the whale blows air through them, creating a mind-boggling noise that can be heard 8 km (5 miles) away.

Basking shark: close to 14 m (45 ft) long, estimated 32,500 kg (32 tons)—about 160 average grown men.

Southern elephant seal: 5.5 m (18 ft)—as long as a full-sized truck.

Sea star: 96 cm (38 inches) in diameter, weighing 5 kg (11 lbs)— as much as a sack of potatoes.

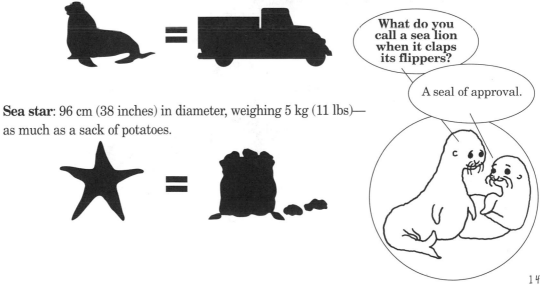

What do you call a sea lion when it claps its flippers?

A seal of approval.

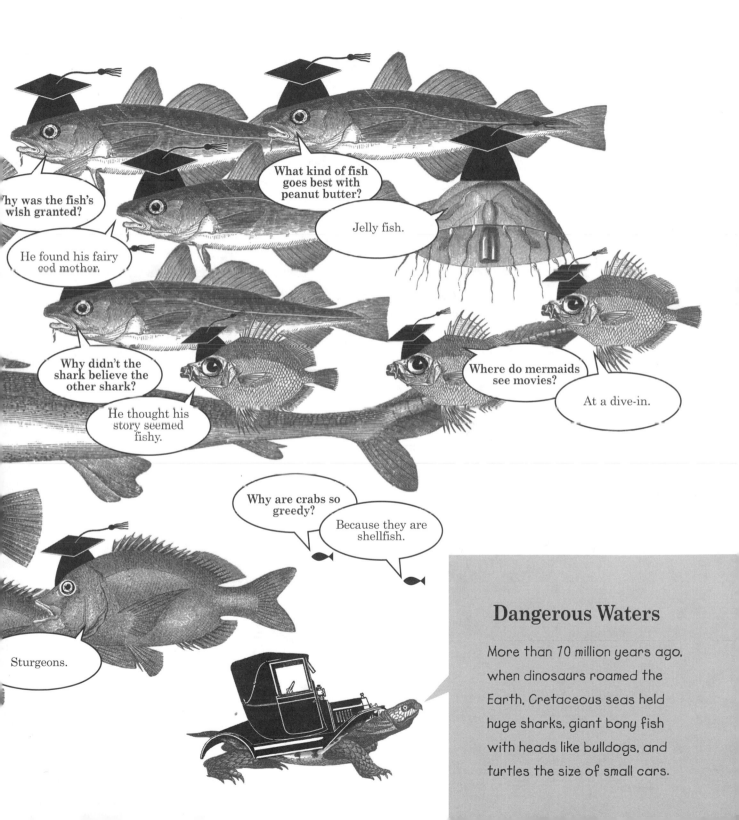

Dangerous Waters

More than 70 million years ago,
when dinosaurs roamed the
Earth, Cretaceous seas held
huge sharks, giant bony fish
with heads like bulldogs, and
turtles the size of small cars.

Wild at Sea

No, the **Portuguese man-of-war** is not a battleship. It looks like a jellyfish, but it consists of four organisms that live together as one. The whole thing grows from a single larva that multiplies into new larvae that become different parts of the colony: one larva becomes the gas-filled flotation device at the top; others become a tentacle and so on. Why the name? The flotation device reminded people of the sails of a Portuguese sailing ship.

• • •

Sea cucumbers have bodies that can grow to be 1 m (3 ft) long. If cut into pieces, each one can become a new sea cucumber.

• • •

You can make two **sponges** out of one—as long as it's alive. When a sponge is divided, its cells will re-grow and combine exactly as before.

• • •

Sea stars that lose arms can grow new ones; sometimes an entire animal can grow from a single lost arm.

The Shocking Truth

There are many kinds of fish that can emit electrical shocks. The most powerful shock is from an electric eel found in South American rivers that can stun a large animal with its electricity!

EYE, EYE, SAILOR

Scientists have recently discovered that the **brittlestar** sea star is covered with tiny light-collecting lenses all over its body. These microlenses are about half as wide as a human hair, and together they act as one big eye. Scientists hope that studying these microlenses could reveal information to help develop optical networks and microchip production.

On dark nights, you may have seen glow-worms or fireflies flashing on and off. The chemical process that creatures use to glow is called **bioluminescence**. But did you know that most of these talented creatures live underwater? Biologists believe that there are at least 1,000 species of bioluminescent squid and fish.

Sailing the Seas

Or, at least, sailors used to tell these myths and beliefs:

Black cats brought bad luck in the form of storms and hurricanes.

A **rabbit's foot** was good luck.

But if a **live rabbit** was on board the ship, it was sure to bring tragedy.

Barnacles on the sides of ships could transform into birds.

If a sailor saw a **crossed-eyed woman**, it was bound to bring bad luck.

Under the seaweed of the Sargasso Sea lived the sons of **Neptune**, the Greek god who ruled the sea. Any sailor going on this sea would meet an early death.

That was once the scariest call heard in the British Isles. It meant that the **Viking** ships had been seen off the coast and soon big men in fast ships would arrive to raid rich monasteries, burn towns and carry off treasure and captives.

• • •

The **Roskilde Dragon** ship was a Viking longship 35 m (115 ft) long that carried 60 fierce warriors. She was built of oak in the reign of King Canute, about 1,000 years ago.

• • •

Horns on their **helmets**? Never! Horns could catch a sword and the helmet could get ripped off your head, when the whole point was to keep it on for protection!

• • •

Some people still think that Columbus discovered America. But the Viking **Leif Erikson** reached America from Greenland in the year 1001 A.D. We also know that the Vikings settled in Newfoundland, which they called Vinland. The whole story is told in the Norse Sagas, but apparently in Columbus' time nobody in the rest of Europe ever read them.

MYSTERY SEA

The **Bermuda Triangle** is a mysterious part of the Atlantic Ocean, bordered by lines from Miami to Bermuda, Bermuda to Puerto Rico, and Puerto Rico to Miami. There are many stories of boats, ships, and planes disappearing in the triangle, never to be seen again. Most of the triangle is a part of the Sargasso Sea, and way before all the talk about the Bermuda Triangle, ships were found deserted in the Sargasso Sea.

• • •

There is a species of **seaweed** that grows in this massive area, floating like a strange forest hundreds of miles from land.

• • •

The Bermuda Triangle is surrounded by some of the strongest sea **currents** in the world — the Florida, Gulf Stream, Canary, North Equatorial, Antilles, and Caribbean.

What musical instrument from Spain helps you fish?

A cast-a-net.

Do you know what is the windiest place on the planet? Or how loud a thunderclap is? What about the difference between a hurricane and a tornado? From rain and snow to tsunamis, the following pages give you the low-down on what might be happening outside your window. You'll even find out some of the ways that animals can clue us in to what weather is on its way. So grab your umbrella, put on your snowshoes, and let's go looking for that next storm!

Weather Forecast

Who Has Seen the Wind?

UNDER PRESSURE

Your weather report talks about areas of high and low pressure, but did you know that this is what causes wind? In areas of high pressure, the air molecules are jammed close together. The air moves from areas of **high** pressure to areas of **low** pressure, like the air rushing out of a balloon—and that's wind.

HIGH WINDS

You'd want to hold on to more than your hat if you felt this. One of the **highest wind speeds** recorded in the U.S. was on Mount Washington, New Hampshire, in 1934. The wind hit a speed of 369.6 km/h (230 mph)—that's almost as fast as the record speed for a helicopter!

• • •

Even faster winds were recorded when a series of **tornadoes** hit Oklahoma in May of 1999. Winds of 511 km/h (318 mph) were blowing—that's the fastest speed you can reach on a motorcycle.

• • •

The windiest place on Earth is **Antarctica**. The winds average 65 km/h (40 mph) throughout the year, but have reached 174 km/h (108 mph). Compare those speeds to how fast a car goes.

Chase that Twister!

Some people—known as storm chasers—will drive all the way across the country just to watch clouds turn black, lightning strike, and finally the frightening funnel of a twister as it touches the ground.

TWISTER!

Tornadoes are nature's most violent storms. A tornado is a violent rotating column or snake of air coming down from a thunderstorm to the ground. As it races over land, it picks up debris, animals, people, and cars—and extremely violent ones destroy homes.

• • •

Some can reach wind speeds of 400 km/h (250 mph) and more.

• • •

Tornadoes cause damage when they touch down on the ground.

• • •

Less than 2% of tornadoes are really destructive.

• • •

The whirling winds of a tornado circle tighter and tighter until they are concentrated into a small area. That's why they are called twisters.

• • •

In the United States in 1874, a series of 148 tornadoes struck 13 states. Hundreds of people died and thousands were injured along its damage path—at over 4,000 km (2,500 miles), about the same distance as the width of the entire country.

What happened when the dairy barn was carried away by the tornado?

Udder disaster!

Wind and Waves

HURRICANE WATCH

A **hurricane** (called a typhoon or cyclone in some parts of the world) is a storm that has developed over warm tropical waters. The combined actions of air, water, and heat produce a massive spinning system of clouds and wind.

● ● ●

Strangely, right in the center of a hurricane there is an area of total calm where there is no wind at all. This is called the **eye of the storm**.

● ● ●

Hurricane hunters are professional pilots and scientists who risk their lives by flying into the eye of a hurricane. Their high-flying aircraft are meteorological stations equipped with special sensors that collect information and send it to the U.S. National Hurricane Center in Florida.

A Him- or a Her-icane?
Hurricanes are given names, like people. The first storm of the year always starts with the letter A, the second one with B and so on. All hurricanes used to have girls' names, but now they alternate between male and female names.

WAVE HELLO!

A **tsunami** (from the Japanese for "harbor wave") is a series of gigantic waves that follow an undersea disturbance, usually an earthquake. Just the way a stone thrown into water causes ripples, tsunami waves move outward in many directions. Up to 30 m (100 ft) high— that's about as high as the Wright brothers flew in the first airplane flight—they travel at speeds up to 725 km/h (450 mph). When the waves hit land, the destruction begins.

In 1806, Admiral Sir Francis Beaufort of the British Navy developed a method to identify wind force. Still used today, the Beaufort Wind Speed Scale measures winds from **Calm** to **Hurricane**.

Beaufort Force Number 3 is termed a **Gentle Breeze**: on land, leaves are in motion; at sea there are large wavelets, crests begin to break and scattered whitecaps appear.

The term **Hurricane**—at Beaufort Force Number 17—tips the scale with violent movements of trees and much destruction on land. At sea, the air is filled with foam, the sea is completely white with driving spray, and visibility is greatly reduced.

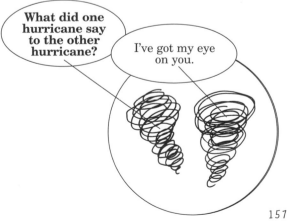

What did one hurricane say to the other hurricane?

I've got my eye on you.

Lightning and Thunder

LIGHTNING STRIKES

During a thunderstorm, storm clouds become electrically charged. When there is a great enough difference in charge between the cloud and its surroundings, the cloud discharges a lightning bolt.

• • •

According to scientists, lightning **smells**! The smell comes from two chemical reactions (which, incidentally, are good for crops)—one that turns oxygen into ozone, and another that forms nitrous oxides.

• • •

Around the Earth, there are 100 lightning strikes **per second**. That works out to 8,640,000 times per day.

• • •

Got **static** during a storm? Your radio or TV is picking up on lightning strikes between the clouds and the ground.

Hot Flash!
The temperature of a typical lightning bolt is hotter than the surface of the Sun.

THUNDER CLAPS

A lightning bolt heats the air around it, which instantly expands, sending out a vibration or shock wave we hear as an explosion of sound. This is **thunder**.

● ● ●

If you are near the stroke of lightning, you'll hear thunder as one sharp **crack**. When lightning is far away, thunder sounds more like a low **rumble** as the sound waves echo off hillsides, buildings, and trees.

● ● ●

A thunderclap can register around 120 decibels, which is enough to make cats and dogs scamper for cover. The noise is about twice that of a pneumatic drill and louder than a chainsaw.

● ● ●

There is an old superstition that thunder makes milk go sour! It is not true, but it might come from the fact that thunderstorms are common in hot, humid weather, when unrefrigerated milk goes sour more quickly anyway.

the calm the storm

What familiar saying does this word puzzle represent?

Answer:
The calm before the storm.

The Sky Is Falling

RAINY DAY PEOPLE

Dark clouds are usually **storm clouds**, which have a high ice-crystal content. Light has difficulty passing through them so they appear dark. Each holds about 6 trillion raindrops.

• • •

A **raindrop** can fall from the sky between 3 and 9 m (10–30 ft) a second. That's fast! But most raindrops are so small—around the thickness of a coin—they won't whack your head too hard.

• • •

Every minute of the day about 1 billion tonnes (907 million tons) of **rain** falls on Earth—about the same weight as 10,000 oil tankers!

• • •

Raining cats and dogs? It's more likely to rain **fish** or **frogs**. Most often, these creatures are picked up from the ground by a tornado and then dropped elsewhere. In fact, it once rained maggots in Mexico and minnows in Scotland. Yuck—you'd definitely need an umbrella for those.

Time to Find the Pot of Gold

Since they change as the sun moves, most rainbows last only about 30 minutes. But in North Wales, there was a day in 1979 with a rainbow that lasted three whole hours.

LET IT SNOW

Snowflakes are formed when ice crystals form on dust particles as water vapor condenses, and partially melted crystals cling together to form snowflakes.

Most snowflakes are less than 1 cm (½ inch) across, but snowflakes about 5 cm (2 inches) wide have been seen.

• • •

A snowflake was once measured at about 38 cm (15 inches) across—about the size of your average dinner plate. It was probably a whole collection of flakes that joined together on the way down.

• • •

When it's very cold and snowing, the flakes are small, and when it warms up closer to freezing, the flakes are larger.

• • •

The highest recorded snowfall in just 24 hours was in Silver Lake, Colorado, in 1921 when nearly 2 m (6 ½ ft) fell. That's enough to cover the head of a tall man standing up.

What do you get when two meteorologists each break an arm and a leg?

Four casts!

Furred and Feathered Forecasters

Many people think that animals and plants can predict the weather. Some watch for animal behavior that is just plain wacky, but some predictions seem reasonable. What do you think of these folk-wisdom forecasts?

If **swans** fly toward the wind, it means a hurricane in 24 hours.

• • •

Crickets chirp faster when the temperature rises.

• • •

Swallows flying low indicate the air pressure is dropping.

• • •

Cows lie down when it is going to rain. The air pressure might affect their digestive systems, and it is easier to lie than stand.

• • •

Some **flowers** close up when humidity rises—possibly so that the rain doesn't wash their pollen away.

• • •

Some **leaves** on trees curl just before a storm.

• • •

When an earthquake is approaching, **fish** swim around in circles in ponds and rivers, and deep-sea fish that can't be caught normally are caught.

• • •

If **fish** jump out of the water, rain is coming. Maybe they leap to catch insects that are flying lower because their wings are weighed down with the damp.

• • •

If a **snowshoe hare** leaves wide footprints in the fall—with extra-furry feet—it means that there will be heavy snowfalls.

Living Fog Machines
Animals making weather? Well, not quite, but herds of caribou in Canada's North can make their own fog on very cold days. When they breathe out, the moisture in their breath creates a fog around them!

Some say: the louder the frog, the more the rain. And if a rooster crows during the rain, the rain will stop before the night.

What's At the End of the Rainbow?

The other end of the rainbow. Although rainbows look like arcs, they are actually round, forming a colored light ring opposite the Sun. They seem like arcs because most of the time the bottom half is blocked by the horizon so we only see part of the rainbow.

Can February March?
No, but April May.

Why was 6 afraid of 7?
Because 7 8 9.

What gets wetter the more you dry?
A towel.

Why do you have to be careful with sunrises and sunsets?
Because day breaks and night falls.

Which kind of house weighs the least?
A lighthouse.

What's full of holes but holds water?
A sponge.

What are two things you can't eat for breakfast?
Lunch and dinner.

What's round and bad-tempered?
A vicious circle.

Why did the judge send the turtle to jail?
Because he was known as a hard case.

Have you heard the joke about the jump rope?
Skip it.

Why are pianos hard to open?
Because the keys don't open locks.

Why is a slippery sidewalk like music?
If you don't C Sharp, you'll B Flat.

What works only after it's been fired?
A rocket.

Which month of the year has 26 days?
All of them.

How many books can you carry in an empty backpack?
None. The backpack's empty!

What can you put into a barrel full of water to make it lighter?
A hole.

OK, I've seen birds and planes...but what are you doing here?

Which bird is always out of breath? *A puffin.* Who didn't invent the airplane? *The Wrong Brothers.* What's an astronaut's favorite drink? *Gravi-tea.* From the flight of the, well, fly, to the birds that soar as high as Mount Everest, the next pages will tell you about all kinds of amazing things that happen in the air. Birds can fly backwards, fragile butterflies can travel across the globe, and humans take the adventure even further—right out into space!

In the Air

For the Birds

BIGGEST

What weighs 12 kg (25 lbs), has a wingspan of 3 m (10 ft), and flies? Something from the prehistoric ages? No, it's the **Andean condor**, the world's largest bird of prey.

SMALLEST

The smallest bird in the world—the **bee hummingbird** of Cuba—also builds the smallest nest of all. It's no bigger than a thimble. The **vervain hummingbird** of Jamaica lays pea-sized eggs—the smallest in the world.

MOST VERSATILE

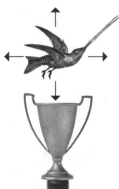

The **hummingbird** can fly backwards—the only bird in the world that can. It can also hover and fly straight up or down. Do hummingbirds hum? No. The hum is the noise made by their wings.

HIGHEST FLYER

In 1967 an airline pilot was surprised to see 30 **whooper swans** outside his window. He—and they—were flying at 8,230 m (27,000 ft), about as high as Mount Everest.

LOUDEST FLAPPER

The beating wings of the **great pied hornbill** are so loud that they can be heard almost 1 km (more than ½ mile) away. It is said to make a chug-chug sound like a steam train.

FASTEST FLAPPER

A close race—what a flap! Some kinds of hummingbirds flap their wings almost 100 times per second. The **horned sungem** of tropical South America can flap its wings 90 times a second.

Arctic tern is out of the country and is unavailable to accept this award in person.

BEST TRAVELED

The **Arctic tern** likes to spend the northern summer in the Arctic and the southern summer in the Antarctic. So every year it flies half way round the world—and back. That's about 17,500 km (10,800 miles) each way. Since an Arctic tern can live to be 30 years old, in its lifetime this little bird can travel over a million kilometers!

BIGGEST WINGSPAN

A big wave to the **wandering albatross**. It has a wingspan longer than a ping pong table.

THE FASTEST

The **white-throated spine-tailed swift** soars to first place as fastest bird at 169 km/h (105 mph). They are also really high flyers, sleeping at heights of 2,100 m (6,500 ft), and even mating in the air!

Z z z z z z z z z

Flying in Its Sleep
An albatross can sleep while it flies. It dozes while cruising at 40 km/h (25 mph).

Why do birds fly south for the winter?

It's easier than walking.

Where do birds invest their money?

In the stork market.

What do birds use for skydiving?

Sparrow-chutes.

Hang on Tight!

Why don't birds fall off their perches when they sleep? They have handy little tendons in their legs. When sleeping or resting, the bird bends its knees, pulling the tendons really tight. This tightening closes the claws, so they grip tightly onto the branch.

Where does a bird go when it loses its tail?

The re-tail store.

Why does a flamingo stand on one leg?

Because if it lifted the other one, it would fall over!

Insect Flight

BUTTERFLIES FLUTTER BY

The **monarch butterfly** has been recorded traveling 2,900 km (1,800 miles) from the northern United States to its winter home near Mexico City.

• • •

Even with its wings outstretched, the **dwarf blue butterfly** of South Africa could barely cover a penny.

• • •

A butterfly flaps its wings about 300 times a minute—five times a second.

• • •

Butterflies never grow. They come out of their chrysalis at full size.

TO BEE, OR NOT TO BEE

A bee traveling at cruising speed could go 1,700,000 km (1,056,000 miles) on 1 liter (1 quart) of nectar—if it didn't get too tired. How's that for fuel efficiency?

• • •

About 80,000 bees must fly the equivalent of three times around the world to gather the nectar for a large jar of honey for your toast.

• • •

Unlike most bees, the **mason bee** lives alone. It lays individual eggs in a mud-walled cell that it builds and supplies with pollen and nectar.

• • •

During hot weather, bees have do-it-yourself air conditioning. Worker bees bring drops of water inside the hive, then fan their wings over the water to evaporate it and cool the air. How's that for bee a/c?

Bug Lights
About 40 fireflies in a dark room will make enough light to read by.

Nothing flies better than…a **fly**. It flies fast and nimble, thanks to a short structure called a haltere behind each wing. The halteres can vibrate 200 times a second, sending messages to the fly's brain that let it automatically make course and speed changes while it is flying.

Going Batty

Bats are the only **mammal** that
possess wings and can truly fly.

• • •

The world's largest known bat colony is found
in the **Bracken Cave** near San Antonio, Texas.
There are estimated to be 20 million or more hanging in there.

• • •

Vampire bats need a nightly meal of blood. If they go two nights
in a row without eating, they will die. They lick animal blood from little
punctures they make with their teeth.

• • •

Australia has some of the world's largest fruit bats and some of the
smallest too. Imagine seeing a **flying fox**, with a wingspan of about 1 m
(3 ft), zooming overhead. Compare this with the **blossom bat**, which is about
the size of your thumb.

• • •

Although no one knows for sure, scientists think that the oddly shaped nose of the
leaf-nosed bat is like a bit of modern technology. It might be a sort of dish antenna
to pick up sonar echoes from flying insects.

Baby bats are called **pups**. A mother bat can locate her pup in a group of thousands of bats. She uses her keen sense of smell to find her baby by its own distinctive scent.

Most bats would be miserable in the water—but not the **fruit bat**. It uses its strong wings to skim along in a bat version of the butterfly stroke.

• • •

The phrase "blind as a bat" is a myth. All bats have some vision, and many can see fine in the daylight. Some bats use a better method than seeing to find prey at night. It is called **echolocation**; the bat sends out a high-pitched squeak that bounces off the bat's prey then echoes back to tell the bat where the food is.

What do bats spend a lot ot time doing?

Answer:
Hanging around upside down.

175

Out of the Air

When you hear the word "bird," the first thing you think about is flight, right? But some birds are flightless:

Rheas are large South American birds similar to ostriches. Rhea fathers take total care of the babies. From the time they are eggs until they are able to survive on their own, he will feed and protect them.

● ● ●

The **roadrunner**—yes, like the one in the cartoon—prefers to run rather than fly. It can go about 37 km/h (23 mph) to catch prey such as lizards and snakes.

If **penguins** are stuck standing on the ice, how come they don't get cold feet? Because they have learned how to control the flow of blood to their feet! In cold weather, the flow of blood is reduced and in warmer weather the flow increases.

● ● ●

The **kakapo** from New Zealand is the world's rarest, largest, and weirdest parrot. It is flightless, nocturnal, and weighs about as much as a rabbit. Unfortunately, out of the hundreds of thousands that used to exist, there are now only 86 of these birds left in the world.

● ● ●

A **kiwi** is more than a fruit. The bird kind is about the size of a chicken, tailless, and with tiny wings that are no good for flying. It looks pretty useless, but a kiwi can run faster than you. And stay out of the way of its sharp toes, which it uses to kick and slash at enemies.

Sorry, I'll be spending Thanksgiving in Mauritius this year.

Ssssssoaring Sssssnakes

Imagine snakes that fly—well, glide—from tree to tree! Some tree snakes from South and Southeast Asia take off from a high place, wriggling into an "S" shape and flattening their bodies out to soar to the ground or another tree.

GONE THE WAY OF THE DODO

The **dodo** or **tambalacoque tree**, which grows on the island of Mauritius off the east coast of Africa, was nearly extinct until a few years ago. Dodos—big flightless birds that have been extinct for some time—used to eat the fruits of the tree, allowing the seeds to start to sprout. But without the dodo to help, by 1970 there were only 13 tambalacoque trees left. Trying to figure out a way to save them from being "dead as a dodo," scientists came up with the **turkey**! In some ways, turkeys are similar to the extinct dodo, and even though they don't like the fruit of the dodo tree, they do eat the pits. So now there are new seedlings growing and the turkey has saved the dodo tree!

How do toads fly?

By hopper-craft.

177

Going My Way?

Around 100 million waterfowl migrate from Canada to the warmer climates of the southern United States and Central and South America each fall. Scientists know that many different waterfowl use the same four major "flyroutes" to head south for the winter. Although they don't know exactly how these birds find their way, scientists believe that some of these routes have been used for more than a million years!

What bird is always in the kitchen?

A cook-oo.

What bird can write under water?

A ball-point pen-guin.

What did the cuckoo say when it fell off a branch?

Cuck-plop.

What kind of movies do ducks like best?

Duck-umentaries.

What time does a duck wake up?

At the quack of dawn.

Human Airheads

Bicycle Built for...Flight

Remember the scene in the movie *E.T.* when the kids pedal their bicycles into the air? Joe Zinni did the same thing in 1976, pedaling his way into history as the first American ever to achieve man-powered flight. Instead of a wheel, the pedals drove a propeller, and Joe's bike-like plane had long wings. The flight lasted about half a minute.

AIRSHIP FRIENDSHIP

Airships are lighter-than-air craft that float in the air for the same reason that party balloons do—they are filled with helium gas, which is lighter than air.

• • •

Unlike balloons, airships have engines and controls, so they can fly where the pilots want them to go.

• • •

Blimps are a type of airship. Did you know that the first aircraft to fly over the North Pole was an airship from Italy? Bigger airships once carried passengers across the Atlantic.

• • •

Airships are pretty slow but unlike airplanes, which burn fuel to fly, they can stay aloft for days on the same helium gas.

The rate of descent for a traditional parachute is about 5.5 m (18 ft) per second.

'CHUTING FOR THE SKY

Brilliant artist and inventor Leonardo da Vinci designed a **parachute** in 1495, but it wasn't used because they didn't have planes back then.

● ● ●

The first military parachutes were designed to save pilots who had to jump from damaged aircraft.

● ● ●

Skydivers wear two parachutes, one on their back and another one on their chest—just in case the first one doesn't work.

● ● ●

When a skydiver pulls the ripcord, the holder of the back parachute splits open. A little parachute called the pilot 'chute pops out and drags the main parachute—the canopy—all the way open. Fully open, a parachute becomes a sort of umbrella with a series of cords that the parachutist pulls on to control the direction of his or her fall.

Who didn't invent the airplane?

The Wrong Brothers.

What is a Mach?

Ernst Mach first compared the speed of an object to the speed of sound—1,234.8 km/h (760 mph), which he called MACH 1. Twice the speed of sound is MACH 2. So, if you are piloting a plane at half the speed of sound, you are flying at MACH .5.

The Final Frontier

Sunrise, Sunset
If you were on the International Space Station, you'd see the Sun rise 16 times a day. And set, too! Why? Because the Station orbits Earth every 90 minutes, passing from the night side to the day side, and back again.

The first man landed on the Moon in 1969; his name was Neil Armstrong.

WHAT IS THE EARTH'S BIGGEST SATELLITE?

Here are a couple of clues: it was around way before humans ever invented communication satellites, rockets, or space shuttles. You can see it without a telescope, mostly at night, but sometimes you can see it in the day. It's the **Moon**. The Moon is 3,700 km (2,300 miles) across, and, on average, 384,400 km (238,900 miles) away.

• • •

Almost all of the planets in our solar system have moons. But which planet has the most? The planet Jupiter has 39!

• • •

The planet Venus doesn't have a moon. Mars has two, called Deimos and Phobos.

STILL PHONING HOME

The **Voyager space probes** were launched in 1977. Even though they have long since left our solar system, they are still sending messages back to Earth. They are the first machines made by humans to ever travel into the darkness between the stars.

WARM HANDS, FAST JET!

The **SR 71 Blackbird** jet flies in the stratosphere—only one atmosphere layer away from outer space—more than 25 km (82,000 ft) up. We know that it's really cold that high up, with temperatures far below freezing. But the Blackbird is so fast—over MACH 3, or 3 times the speed of sound—that friction heats up the outside of the plane. The pilots can warm their hands on the windows, which are 10 times as thick as regular windows!

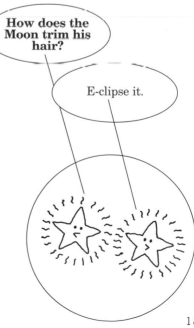

How does the Moon trim his hair?

E-clipse it.

It Came from Outer Space

Did I remember to vacuum before I left home?

VISITORS FROM SPACE?

More than 60 years ago, during World War II, both German and British fighter pilots reported seeing strange glowing balls zipping around their aircraft at night. The pilots, thinking they were high-tech enemy weapons, would try and chase them, but they would vanish as quickly as they had appeared. These strange objects were called **foo fighters**. So, were foo fighters sent by extra-terrestrials? Or were they lightning, unusual electrical optical effects—or simply created by the minds of pilots who were tired and on edge? We may never know.

● ● ●

Stardust isn't just what space aliens sweep up when they clean their ships. Stars sometime explode, and when they do, the fallout scatters into space. Whether in small particles, like the dust in your home, or as big as boulders, stardust either floats to other planets, or comes together in a big enough chunk to form a planet of its own. This might even have been how our Earth was formed. Do you want to see stardust? Just look under the furniture at home. Our planet is still gathering the stardust that floats by in space—about 1 million kg (1,000 tons) of it every day!

Tiny Martians?
Recently a scientist suggested that bacteria, the first forms of life, remain several miles underground in the earth, living on natural oil deposits. He also believes that similar subterranean life might flourish on Mars and other planets.

INTO THE BLACK

What's a **black hole**? Not something you dig—but a strange phenomenon in space that some people think exist, and others don't. Imagine a huge empty space, so dense that not even light can escape the extra-strong pull of its gravity. Getting caught in a black hole would be like falling into a black pit forever—because there's no bottom. Black holes are probably caused when stars more than three times the size of our Sun collapse in on themselves.

• • •

A **neutron star** is a star that doesn't glow. When a star about 3 times the size of our sun burns out, it collapses and is kind of smashed into tiny atoms, mostly particles called neutrons. The neutron star is crushed very small—only about 20 to 30 km (12 to 18 miles) across—and spins very fast. It is very dense and has very strong gravity—sort of a mini-black hole.

What is this?

Answer:
A flying saucer caught on a telephone line.

Do Astronauts Cry?

An astronaut might feel sad, but it's impossible to cry in space. Why? There's no gravity in space so the tears won't flow.

When do you put the cart before the horse? *In the dictionary.* What do you get when you cross a skunk with a vegetable? *Smellery.* What do you get when you cross a supersonic jet with a hamburger? *Very fast food.* Humans are great thinkers—we are always using our brains to invent new things to make our lives easier and more convenient. In the following pages, you'll find out how people came up with things you use everyday—from pizza to video games, from the bicycle to Velcro™. You'll also test your own brain by solving word games, puzzles, and optical illusions.

Who Came Up with That?

Inventive Minds

Sometimes, inventors are trying to invent one thing, and end up inventing something else.

A young chemist at the DuPont company was trying to develop a non-stick chemical for use in refrigerators. What he came up with was non-stick all right, but wasn't exactly what he was trying for. Called **Teflon**®, the space-age material resists corrosion and is a great insulator. Although it has been used for spaceship fuel tanks, space suits, space probes, and satellites, you know it best as the non-stick coating on your pots and pans. Oh, and as the warm, light, and breathable **Gore-Tex**® in your all-weather wear.

Peter Hodgson at General Electric was trying to come up with a rubber substitute. When he combined boric acid and silicone, he got a gooey substance that looked good for nothing. He threw it on the floor—and it bounced right back. Hey, maybe it would make a great toy! He sold it packed in plastic eggs—as **Silly Putty**®.

• • •

In 1942, Dr. Harry Coover was working for the Kodak Research Laboratories, trying to develop an optically clear plastic to use in gun sights. He discovered a substance called cyanoacrylate, that you've used if you ever had to stick a broken toy or mug back together. This sticky stuff is known as **Superglue** or **Krazy Glue**®.

LET THERE BE LIGHTBULBS

If someone asked you who invented the lightbulb, you would probably say it was **Thomas Edison**. And you would be wrong! Back in the late 1800s, about a dozen inventors were working on the idea. Edison was already famous for inventing things. He improved the lightbulb, and then convinced people that his lightbulbs were the best. People took for granted that, if Edison made them, Edison must have invented them.

Nice Going, Kid

In 1873, at the age of 15, Chester Greenwood invented ear muffs. Wanting something better than a scarf wrapped around his head to keep his ears warm, he made two ear-shaped hoops from wire and had his grandmother help him sew fur onto them.

RACE TO GET TO THE PHONE

If **Elisha Gray** had reached the patent office before **Alexander Graham Bell**, he would have been hailed as the inventor of the telephone. It didn't stop Gray taking Bell to court suing for the patent rights. He lost, and Bell is credited with the invention.

POP QUIZ
My name is Wilhelm Conrad Röentgen. In my lab, I found special light rays passed through heavy black cardboard and made a screen across the room glow. What were they?

Answer:
X-rays.

Standing Sticks ▶

Turn the book slightly, so the corner is in front of you, and look at the lines in the direction of the arrow. Now tip it slightly away from you. What happens when you close one eye and look at the lines? Do the lines look like they are standing straight up off the page?

◀ One Cube or Two?

There are two cubes in the picture at left, but you can only see one cube at a time. Which one you see all depends on which corner of the white side your brain thinks is closer to you. Which cube do you see first?

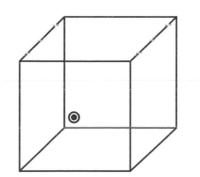

Floating Balls

What happens when you stare at this picture for a few seconds? The balls come to life. The light-colored balls seem to rise up from the page. The shadow beneath makes this more realistic by giving the balls depth.

Face to Face ▶

Look at the dot in this box. Is it at the front of the cube or at the back? Are you sure?

1961

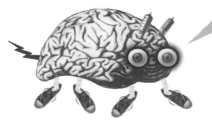

An Unusual Year

The year 1961 has an unusual distinction. Have you figured out what that is? Hint: Turn the book so you can look at this page upside down. What you'll discover is that 1961 upside down is still 1961! We'll have to wait a very, very long time until that happens again. The next time this will be true will be in the year 6009.

Tall Tales *by* A. Lyre

Winter Hikes *by* I. C. Toes

Statues
by Stan Dingstill

Out of Breath
by Ima Puffing

Dieting
by Les Tooeet

Shell Collecting
by Sandy C. Shore

Be Prepared
by Justin Case

Baseball
by A. Diamond

Credit Cards
by Bill Melater

Watering Hole
by O. Asis

Frisbee
by Iman Orb

GLUE Stick Ing

Dinner Delight *by* Roland Butter

The Contest *by* Willie Winn and Betty Can

The
Contest

by
Willie Winn
and Betty Can

The Haunted House
by Hugo First

What is the only word in the dictionary that's spelled incorrectly?

Incorrectly.

What's at the end of everything?

The letter G.

Which two days of the week start with T?

Today and tomorrow.

What time is spelled the same backwards as it is forwards?

Noon.

What's at the end of a rainbow?

The letter W.

How is the letter D like a bad child?

Because it makes ma mad.

Why is the letter T like a cold day?

Because it's in the middle of winter.

What word becomes shorter if you add two letters to it?

Short.

When do you put the cart before the horse?

In the dictionary.

Which letter is found in a cup?

The letter T.

Which two letters of the alphabet contain nothing?

What has two eyes but can't see?

An icicle.

What's in the middle of America and Australia?

The letter R.

How do you spell hard water with three letters?

What occurs once in a minute, twice in a moment, but never in a day?

The letter M.

What 4 letters does the dentist say to her patient?

ICDK
(I see decay).

What has more letters than the alphabet?

The post office.

What's an Acronym?

It's a combination of letters or syllables that make a simple, pronounceable word from a series of words. Here are some well-known words: SCUBA (Self-Contained Underwater Breathing Apparatus), RADAR (Radio Detection and Ranging), and LASER (Light Amplification by the Stimulated Emission of Radiation).

Lazy Phrases

Can you figure out these word puzzles? (*Hint:* Sometimes it helps to solve them if you talk out loud.)

UJUSTS

Answer: Just between us

MOMANON

Answer: Man in the Moon

WOLF

Answer: Lone wolf

AHIBVE

Answer: Bee in a hive

BECOME
CONFIDENT

Answer: Become over-confident

B
O
B

Answer: Bob up and down

BAD WOLF

Answer: Big bad wolf

ECNALG

Answer: Backward glance

N N N N Land

Answer: Foreign (4 N) land

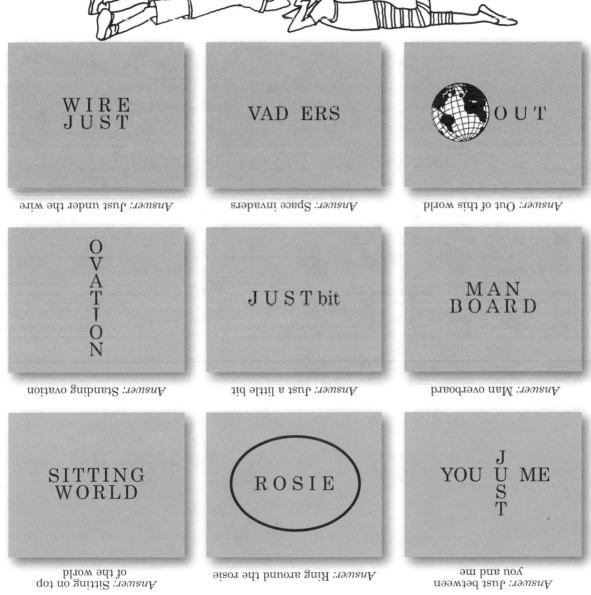

WIRE
JUST

Answer: Just under the wire

VAD ERS

Answer: Space invaders

🌐 **OUT**

Answer: Out of this world

O V A T I O N (vertical)

Answer: Standing ovation

JUST bit

Answer: Just a little bit

MAN
BOARD

Answer: Man overboard

SITTING
WORLD

Answer: Sitting on top of the world

ROSIE (inside circle)

Answer: Ring around the rosie

YOU JUST ME (JUST vertical)

Answer: Just between you and me

Which central circle is larger, the one on the left or the one on the right? You may have guessed the right answer already. They're the same size. The perspective just changes with the size of the other shapes that surround the central circle.

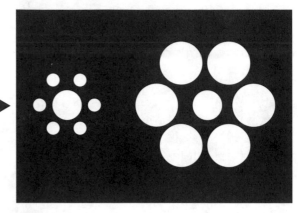

Are the horizontal lines parallel? Believe it or not, they are. You can test them with a ruler or another straight edge.

Study this figure for a few seconds. What do you see? A white vase, or two black faces?

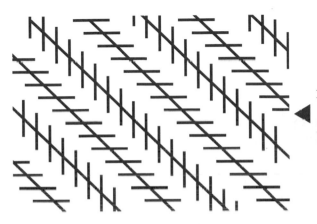

Are the longer diagonal lines parallel? Yes, indeed. Those smaller lines drawn across are just trying to make our brains believe otherwise.

Look closely at the square. Do the lines appear to be wavy? By now you know not to be fooled by appearances. Your trusty ruler will show you that the lines of the square are all straight. The background lines put a different twist on things, though.

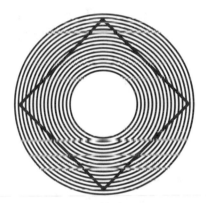

Lefty or Righty?

Nine people out of ten are right-handed. And some people—but very few—are ambidextrous (that means they can use either hand to do the same task). Other people are mixed-handed, meaning they can do different tasks with different hands.

Fun and Games

GO VIDEO

Way back in the 19th century, a Japanese company called Marufuku made and distributed Japanese playing cards. In 1907, it began making Western-style playing cards, and in 1961 changed its name to the Japanese for "leave luck to heaven"—**Nintendo**!

● ● ●

In the 1950s, David Rosen noticed that coin-operated games on American military bases in Japan were very popular, so he started a company called Service Games. At first, Service Games imported new games, but soon Rosen decided to make his own. He purchased a company in Tokyo that manufactured jukeboxes and slot machines. Can you guess what Service Games was shortened to? Yes, you know David Rosen's company as **Sega**.

● ● ●

Ever heard of **Pong**? It was the first successful arcade video game, and was produced in 1974. It more or less created the arcade video game industry. And then Pong was also made as a home video game.

● ● ●

The **Star Wars**® video game was released in 1983. To date, more games have been made of *Star Wars* than any other movie.

Ultimate Fact Guys

Two young Canadian journalists were having a friendly argument about which one knew more about all sorts of things—which led to the invention of Trivial Pursuit®. To date, more than 88 million Trivial Pursuit® board games have been sold.

BARBIE™ WORLD

Ruth Handler, a co-founder of the Mattel Company, invented Barbie™ in 1959.

• • •

Barbie™ was named after Ruth Handler's daughter Barbara. Later, when the Ken doll came along, he was named after her son.

• • •

The first Barbie™ doll sold for $3.00, wearing a black and white swimsuit—and a ponytail.

• • •

Although Barbie™ has had about 80 different careers, she didn't go to college until 1964.

• • •

If all the dolls of Barbie™ and her family members that have been sold since 1959 were placed head to toe, they would circle the earth more than seven times.

• • •

Forty-five different Barbie™ nationalities have been produced.

• • •

Barbie's™ full name is Barbara Millicent Roberts. She is from Willows, Wisconsin.

What is this?

Answer:
A spider doing a handstand.

Visual Games

How many squares can you count in this picture?

Don't peek at the answers on the next page until you're done.

1.

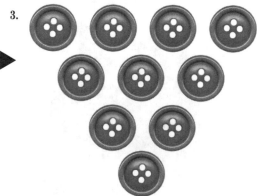

2.

Parents' Land

A couple has a large piece of land that they wish to sell. They want to keep an area for themselves (see area marked off in the diagram) and divide the remaining land into four equal parts for their children. How can they divide the land into four plots of equal shape and size?

Can you make this pyramid of buttons turn upside down by moving only three buttons? Hint: You might want to collect 10 coins or buttons and build this shape to try out different options if you're having difficulty figuring it out just in your head.

3.

A.   B.   C.   D.   E.

Can you "spot" the ladybugs? Using the following 3 clues, you should be able to figure out how many spots each ladybug has.

1. If a ladybug has an even number of spots, then the one to her right will have 1 more spot than she has.
2. If a ladybug has an odd number of spots, then the 1 to her right will have 3 more spots than she has.
3. Each ladybug has at least 1 spot.

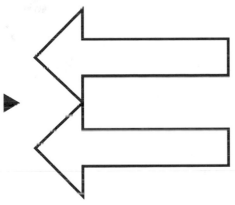

Copy these 2 arrows onto another piece of paper. Then, using only 2 straight lines, can you make a third arrow.

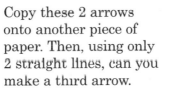

You'll need 12 matches or straws for this puzzle. Set them up like this. By moving only 3 matches or straws, can you make 3 equal squares?

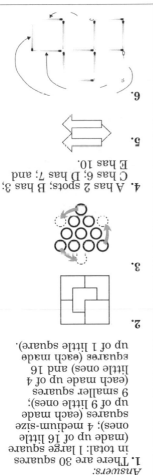

Answers:

1. There are 30 squares in total: 1 large square (made up of 16 little ones); 4 medium-size squares (each made up of 9 little ones); 9 smaller squares (each made up of 4 little ones); and 16 squares (each made up of 1 little square).

2.

3.

4. A has 2 spots; B has 3; C has 6; D has 7; and E has 10.

5.

6.

Fun Food

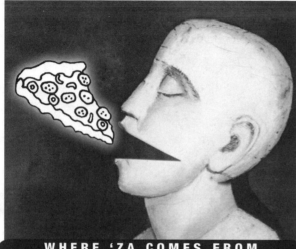

WHERE 'ZA COMES FROM

The **pizza** is really, really old. It was born in Naples during the pre-Renaissance period, about 500 to 700 years ago. Long before that, Roman soldiers were eating something very similar. They would put oil, herbs, and cheese on unleavened bread and bake it on a hearth. The first pizzeria in the U.S.A. opened in New York City in 1905.

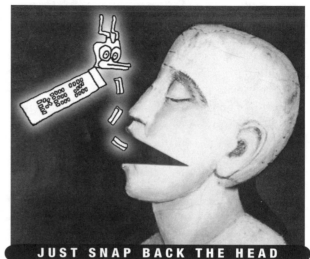

JUST SNAP BACK THE HEAD

Lots of kids collect **PEZ**® dispensers—whether or not they like the little candies inside. The original peppermint PEZ® was sold as an anti-smoking candy. Eduard Haas, an Austrian inventor, invented PEZ® in 1927 and began importing the candy to the U.S.A. in 1952. It didn't sell well until he reinvented it with new fruit flavors and toy dispensers with cartoon heads.

A Nice, Frozen Epsicle?

Frank Epperson, an 11-year-old from San Francisco, got a patent for "frozen ice on a stick" in 1905. He originally called his frozen treat an Epsicle, but the name was changed to Popsicle in 1923.

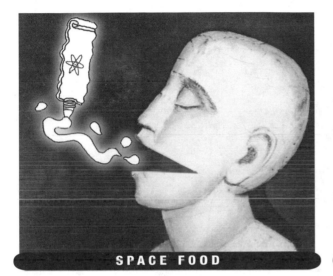

SPACE FOOD

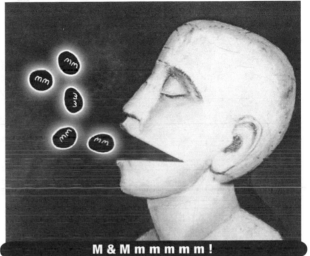

M&Mmmmm!

When John Glenn became the first American astronaut to orbit Earth, one of the things he had to learn was how to eat in a weightless condition. At that time, space food was definitely odd—bite-sized cubes of food, freeze-dried food, and semi-liquids in aluminum toothpaste tubes. Over many years and many space missions, the food became better and easier to handle. Food containers were aluminum cans with pullout lids. Cans had built-in membranes so food wouldn't spill, and instead of plastic bags, collapsible bottles held the drinks. Even eating became normal, with a knife, fork, and spoon held magnetically to the food tray. But astronauts still had to be careful that the food didn't float right off the tray!

How many different colors do **M&M's**® chocolate candies come in? The traditional colors are brown, red, green, yellow and orange. In the early 1980s, packs of seasonal colors went on the market: red and green for Christmas, and pastel colors for Easter. In 1995, blue M&M's® were introduced, and the little candies moved into the 21st century with the introduction of purple!

POP QUIZ

My name is John Pemberton. As a pharmacist, I was trying to make a medicine to make people feel better after having too much to drink. But when my assistant mixed it with carbonated water, it tasted too good to be medicine! What is it?

Answer: Coca-Cola®

Picnic Puzzlers

Where do you weigh a pie?

Somewhere over the rainbow, weigh-a-pie.

A colony of ants was discovered on the Japanese coast containing an estimated one million queens and 306 million workers in 45 interconnected nests! Bet you'd think twice about throwing down your picnic blanket there!

What do you get when you cross a skunk with a vegetable?

Smellery.

Why did the cookie go to see the doctor?

He was feeling crumby.

Who tells the best egg jokes?

A comedi-hen.

What did one plate say to the other plate?

Lunch is on me!

What looks like half a lemon?

The other half.

Why did the tomato blush?

Because it saw the salad dressing.

209

Why couldn't the dessert reach the table?
It was shortbread.

What kind of sandwiches do sailors eat?
Submarines, of course!

What kind of cup can't hold water?
A cupcake.

What do you get when you cross peanut butter and a quilt?
A bread spread.

What did the banana do when the lion roared at it?
It split.

What did the baby corn say to Ma Corn?
Where's Pop Corn?

When does a potato change nationality?
When it's French-fried.

What do you call a green vegetable served on a ship?
A crew-cumber.

The Croc Diet

Up to 60% of a crocodile's food intake can be converted to fat. This makes it able to go a long time between meals. In fact, some large crocodiles have been known to be able to survive up to two years between meals.

If Jack and Jill were a fruit what kind would they be?
A pear.

Why did the tomato go out with the zucchini?
Because he couldn't find a date.

What do you call two banana skins?
Slippers.

Why did the oak tree eat his ice cream out of a dish?
Because the pine tree wouldn't give him a cone.

What's a plumber's favorite vegetable?
Leeks.

What do you call a necklace made of fruit?
A food chain.

A cabbage, a tap, and a tomato were in a race. What happened?
The cabbage was ahead, but the tap kept running, and the tomato was trying to ketchup.

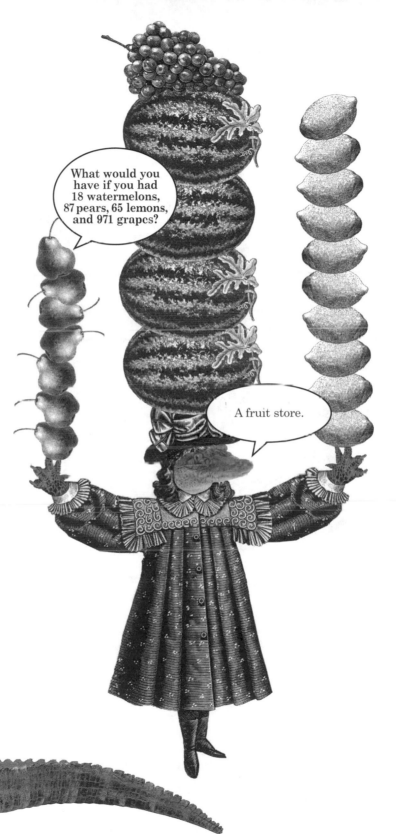

What would you have if you had 18 watermelons, 87 pears, 65 lemons, and 971 grapes?

A fruit store.

211

Which image is on top? Most people see this image as two triangles, one on top of the other, because the triangle is such a familiar shape. Very few people see this as two shapes that are side by side. How do you see it?

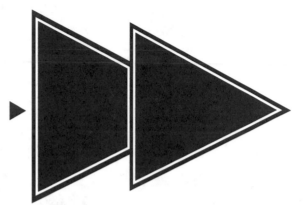

Do you see birds or bunnies, or both?

Is this book opening away from you or toward you? Does it keep changing?

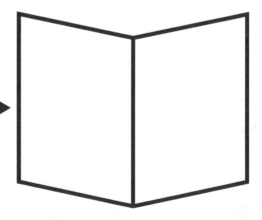

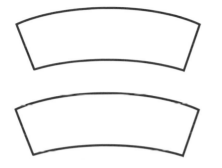

Which of these objects is larger? Actually, they are the same size. The shape on top just looks smaller because its shorter arc is next to the longer arc of the lower figure.

Do you see a triangle in this shape? The shape cut into the circles "tricks" our eye into seeing a triangle here, when in fact there isn't one drawn.

Your Dreaming Brain

Scientists who study brain activity during sleep believe that dreams happen in the right hemisphere of our brains. The left hemisphere is our verbal side. When people say they don't dream, what they really mean is that they don't remember their dreams. Everyone dreams. It just depends from individual to individual whether we are able to transfer the right brain images to the verbal left brain.

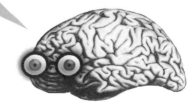

Around the House

STUCK ON YOU

Back in the 1940s, an engineer named George de Mestral and his Irish Pointer dog were in the Swiss Jura mountains. De Mestral had to keep pulling sticky burrs out of his dog's fur, so he took one home and put it under a microscope to see what made it, well, stick. He was amazed to see that the outside of the seedpod was covered with hundreds of tiny hooks that clung like little hands. A little thinking and some work, and he came up with the fabric fastener we know as **Velcro**™—from the French *velour* (velvet) and *crochet* (hook).

● ● ●

How did clear sticky tape come about? Thank Richard G. Drew, an inventor for 3M. Drew's first invention was masking tape to help painters make a straight border. The paper was wide and had adhesive only on the edges of the tape. In 1930 he made an improved tape that was called **Scotch® Brand Cellulose Tape**. The clear, all-purpose adhesive tape was soon being sold worldwide. The first tape dispenser with a cutting edge came about in 1932.

Write Every Mountain

The Parker black ballpoint pen is said to produce more than 8,500 m (28,000 ft) of writing before it runs out—you could draw a line almost as high as Mount Everest!

TOOTHY TRUTHS

Before the invention of the **toothbrush**, humans used sticks with the ends frayed into soft fibers. These were used by the Egyptians as early as 3000 years B.C.

● ● ●

Scientists believe that the Chinese were the first to invent the **bristle brush**; it eventually found its way to Europe in the 17th century.

● ● ●

The first **electric** toothbrushes were used in the U.S.A. in the 1960s.

● ● ●

Before modern **toothpaste** appeared in the 1800s, many different mixtures for cleaning teeth were used all over the world. You might not mind trying powdered fruit, ground shells, honey or dried flowers, but you probably wouldn't want to use a concoction that contained mice or lizard livers!

POP QUIZ

I was working on this chemical to put on aircraft, and now it won't come off my shoe. And that spot isn't getting dirty! What is it?

Answer: Scotchgard™ fabric protector.

Goofy Gadgets Galore

*Some **real** inventions that just never caught on....*

An **umbrella** that informs you if you are leaving it behind.

A motorized **ice-cream cone** that keeps turning around against your tongue.

A drinking **cup** with sound—it burps!

A jet-powered **surfboard**.

BACK TO THE DRAWING BOARD

Patent offices are where inventors can register their ideas so that nobody else can sell them. Here are some ideas that never made it past that point!

Are you pigging out? You could have used the amazing **Alarm Fork**, with a timer and two lights embedded in its handle. Once you've taken a mouthful of food, on pops the red light. Once you've had enough time to properly chew that last mouthful, the green light will come back on and you can eat again!

● ● ●

How about a **glow-in-the-dark toilet** with waterproof lights under the rim of the toilet bowl? Not a bad idea, especially in the middle of the night when you can't find the toilet in the dark.

● ● ●

Here's one for all you girls who tear your pantyhose or tights—**three-legged pantyhose**! You use two legs at a time, and just tuck the other leg away in a handy little pocket. If you damage one leg, don't worry, just pull out the spare one!

● ● ●

What about a **walking stick** with rollers? We've no idea why!

● ● ●

Someone invented a **bed** with rotating canvases at each end, printed with pictures of sheep that you could count if you needed help getting to sleep.

Tongue Twister:
Three fluffy
feathers fell
from Phoebe's
flimsy fan.

Some Truly Useless Inventions
Double-sided playing cards, a black highlighter pen, glow-in-the-dark sunglasses, an inflatable anchor, fireproof matches, a waterproof towel. How many wacky ones can you come up with?

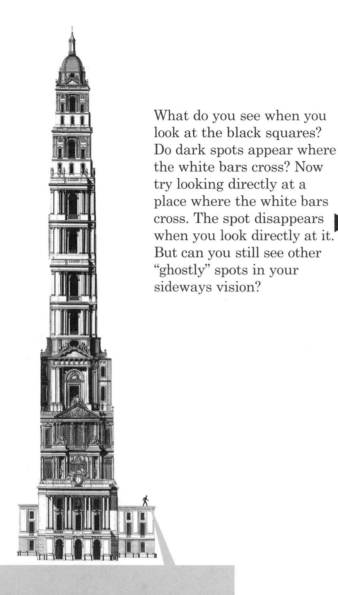

What do you see when you look at the black squares? Do dark spots appear where the white bars cross? Now try looking directly at a place where the white bars cross. The spot disappears when you look directly at it. But can you still see other "ghostly" spots in your sideways vision? ▶

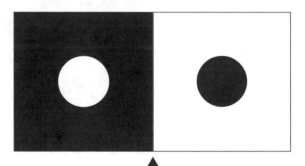

▲

Which circle is bigger, the white one or the black one? If you guessed the white circle you wouldn't be alone. But, you'd actually be wrong. Believe it or not, they're exactly the same size!

How High Is High?

Though these are still only ideas, today's engineers say that within the next 100 years, we will see buildings that are 250 to 500 stories tall! That could be an awfully long elevator ride to the top.

This strange-looking object is called a **blivit**. Look at it carefully. Where is the middle prong attached?

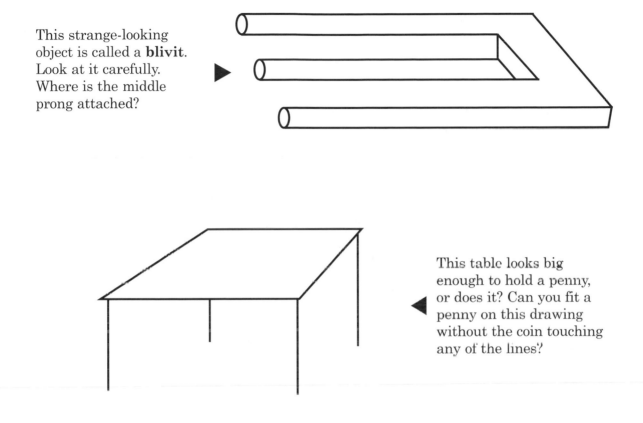

This table looks big enough to hold a penny, or does it? Can you fit a penny on this drawing without the coin touching any of the lines?

Which line is longer, the top or the bottom one? Although most people would say the bottom line looks longer, they're—you guessed it—the exact same length!

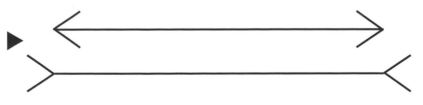

Getting Around

A Frenchman first sold the **bicycle** to the public in 1865. These first bikes on the market were made of heavy wood with an iron frame. Not exactly a smooth ride, these bikes were nicknamed the Boneshaker.

• • •

In peat bogs in the Netherlands, scientists have found 12,000-year-old human skeletons—with animal bone blades tied to their feet. What were they for? Looks like they might have been early **ice skates**!

What does a horse have to do with a car? When Scottish engineer James Watt invented the steam engine in 1775, he wanted to tell people how good his new-fangled machine was. At that time, horses powered the pumps that got water out of coal mines, so Watt compared his engine to the amount of power those horses had—one **horsepower** equals 33,000 foot-pounds per minute.

• • •

Can't read a map? If you were hooked up with a **Global Positioning Satellite**, you would know exactly where on Earth you were at all times. Many modern boats and cars are now equipped with GPS.

Slick-less Quickness
An Enviro-Filter™ fastens to the exhaust of an outboard boat motor and helps catch the oil that would normally go into the water.

Kids all over North America have fold-up **scooters**, but they weren't invented for kids at all. The president of a company in Taiwan wanted to get around his factory faster. This Mr. Tsai worked for 5 years to develop the scooter made of airplane-grade aluminum. When people saw Mr. Tsai zooming around on his scooter, it became the hit of the 1998 World Sports Expo, and now it's worldwide.

All-Purpose Bridge

The Boston Bridge is the only place in the world where you can walk on a bridge, underneath a car bridge, while a train goes over that, while a plane flies above, and boats go underneath.

Computer Terms Glossary!

Analog: What Ana tosses into the fire.
Bandwidth: Limited by the size of the stage.
Cursor: Someone who swears too much.
DAT: The opposite of DIS.
E-mail spam: Lunch delivered through your computer.
Firewall: Stand back, it's hot!
Home computer: What you tell your computer when it follows you to school.
Ink jet: A pen used for skywriting.
Modem: What the gardener did to the lawns.
Motherboard: This happens when you watch cartoons.
Overlay: Chickens making too many eggs.
Reboot: Putting your galoshes on twice.

Smilies

:-)	Happy
:-p	Sticking tongue out
;o)	Wink
:-*	Kiss
:-(	Unhappy
:-x	Keeping a secret
~:o	A baby
=D	Laughing out loud
>:- (	Angry
:-o	Shocked

Internet Abbreviations

BTW	By the way
BFF	Best friends forever
F2F	Face to face (personal meeting)
IMHO	In my humble opinion
BRB	Be right back
MOS	Mom over shoulder
OMG	Oh my gosh
LOL	Laughing out loud
FYI	For your information
IRL	In real life
ROTFL	Rolling on the floor, laughing
THX	Thanks
TTYL	Talk to you later

Bugs!

Mark I, invented in 1944, was the first American general purpose computer controlled by programs. In 1945, Mark II was developed, and during its development, a computer term was coined which is still in use today. After a relay in the computer had failed, scientists discovered the source of the problem: a dead moth inside, which had to be removed. This is thought to be the origin of the word "debugging."

Why don't fish use computers?
They're afraid of getting stuck in the net.

What do computers eat when they get hungry?
Chips.

Why did the computer sneeze?
It had a virus.

What kind of nightclub did the computer go to?
A disk-o.

Why did the computer have to lie down?
It had slipped a disk.

What did the spider do on the computer?
It made a web page.

Why didn't the computer finish its sandwich?
It only wanted a little byte.

Why do cats like computers?
They like playing with the mouse.

What's a computer's favorite sport?
Surfing.

Why did the computer catch a cold?
It forgot to close its windows.

Why was the computer good at golf?

It had a hard drive.

Why did the computer lose its driver's licence?
It was always crashing.

Why was the computer tired when it got home?
Because it had a hard drive.

How does a computer order food?
Off the menu.

What do you get when you cross a computer with a freezer?
Very cool answers.

Why didn't the computer answer the question?
Because it lost its memory.

Hello? Is Anybody Out There?

In the days of the Pony Express, which sent young men on horseback to take mail across the United States, it would take weeks to get word to someone a long way away. Think how amazed someone from that time would be at the ways we communicate over distances!

GETTING WIRED IN THE 20TH CENTURY

The **Internet** had its first beginnings around 1960 when the U.S. Department of Defense wanted a computer network that would still be able to function if one system failed. They created ARPANET to link scientific and academic researchers. In 1985, the National Science Foundation created NSFNET, another series of networks for research and educational communications. Before long, other companies built their own networks that linked to NSFNET.

• • •

Information on those early networks didn't look like the text and images you see on the Internet today. The **World Wide Web** was born in the 1990s when a researcher in Geneva came up with Hyper Text Markup Language (HTML).

WIRELESS...AND WORLDWIDE

Satellites have changed the way just about everything works for us on Earth. Just as Earth goes around—or orbits—the Sun, the Moon is a natural satellite that orbits Earth. Human-made satellites are pieces of machinery sent into orbit to carry out many different functions. A communications satellite transmits TV or telephone signals to Earth.

• • •

Why do we need communications satellites? Because TV and telephone signals are microwaves, and microwaves don't bend. Signals can be sent only between two places in a straight line, and can't follow the curve of the Earth. But a satellite is high enough to be in a straight line from both stations on the ground, so a signal can be shot up from a ground station, received by the satellite and sent back down to a distant ground station.

• • •

EchoStar is one of more than 100 communications satellites orbiting Earth. It is used to send TV signals to homes in North America. EchoStar is in a geosynchronous orbit, which means it stays in exactly one spot over Earth.

Two Tongue Twisters:

World Wide Web, World Wide Web, World Wide Web,....

Flash message, flash message, flash message,....

You didn't think we'd let you sit there and laugh without having to do any work yourself, did you? This book is filled with jokes you can entertain yourself, your friends, and your family with. Here's how to keep the fun going even after you've closed the book. With these tips under your belt, you'll be able to keep coming up with your own brilliant jokes.

Very Punny

A lot of jokes play with words. Your English teacher would call them puns. A pun is a humorous use of a word, which can be taken as having two or more different meanings. Here are some examples:

What did the owl say when he lost his glasses?
He didn't give a hoot.

Why is a fish like someone on a diet?
They both have scales.

How do you do this on your own? Think of an object: a person, place, or thing. Then think of words that are associated with that object. Take a snake, for instance. Words associated with snakes are: slimy, poison, hiss, venom, to name a few. How about:

What's the snake's best subject at school?
Hiss-tory.

How to Make Your Own Jokes

Words that Sound Similar

Words that sound similar to other words but have a different meaning can make clever jokes—like Knock! Knock! jokes. All you have to do is think of a name or an object and think of a word it sounds like. For instance:

> Knock! Knock!
> Who's there?
> **Al.**
> Al who?
> **Al be happy when you open the door and let me in.**

And here's an example of a rhyming word joke:

> **What was the owl's favorite TV show?**
> The feather forecast.

Say What?

Putting together two things that don't usually go together in one joke can make us laugh. Just think of two things you wouldn't associate with each other—for example, a frog and a bicycle—and characteristics of each.

It doesn't have to make sense (in fact, it shouldn't!). You could come up with:

> **What's green and slimy and has two wheels?**
> A frog riding a bicycle.

And here's another:

> **What has red hair and 100 legs?**
> A centipede wearing a wig.

After telling a few jokes like the absurd ones above, you can "trick" people by saying something true or obvious that's not the answer they're expecting to a joke. Here are a few examples, including the most famous one:

> **Why did the chicken cross the road?** To get to the other side.
> **Why did the boy on stilts pick up the phone?** Because it was ringing.
> **What did the cat say to the spider?** Nothing. Cats can't talk.

It's raining cats and dogs

Can you tell which well-known expression each of these drawings illustrates?

Hint: The expressions are listed below.

235

Are you ready?
I am!

Why is it safe to tell a mummy your secrets? *It will keep them under wraps.* What did Frankenstein say to his sweetheart? *It was love at first fright.* What kind of monster loves to disco? *The boogie-man.* These last pages contain some final spooky mysteries, incredible inventions, tips on animal body language, and explanations for a few cryptic sayings. From blood-sucking vampires and ancient excavations to the mysteries of animal feelings, read on for the last, the weirdest, the most wonderful, and the most awesome facts and jokes yet.

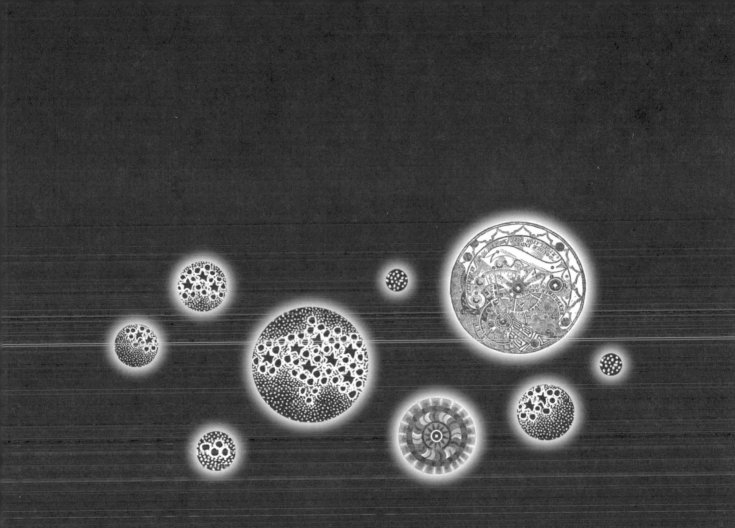

Weird and Wonderful

Very Scary

NOT DEAD YET!

Do you ever wonder where some expressions come from? For example, why does working the "graveyard shift" mean working through the night? And how could someone be "saved by the bell"?

Hundreds of years ago, when there wasn't enough room in the graveyard, old graves were often dug up and re-used. Sometimes the inside of the old coffins showed scratch marks—people had been **buried alive** and tried to get out! How could this have happened? This was before they knew lead was poisonous, and when beer or whisky was drunk out of lead cups. The combination of alcohol and lead sometimes made people unconscious for days. They were often mistaken for dead and quickly buried.

So people came up with the idea of tying a string to the deceased's wrist. The string was pulled out of the coffin and up through the ground, and the end was attached to a bell. Someone would then sit out all night—on the graveyard shift—to listen for a person buried alive to be **saved by the bell.**

DRACULA SUCKS!

Do you know anyone who hasn't heard of the most famous vampire of all? Bram Stoker wrote the book **Dracula** more than a hundred years ago. Since then, there have been countless books and movies about Dracula—and many more fictional vampires have become well known—but none quite so thrilling as the original.

The character of Count Dracula was based on a real man named Prince Vlad III, whose family name was Dracul, or Dragon. Prince Vlad ruled in Transylvania in the 1400s. Because of his nasty habit of killing people in very cruel ways, he was known as Vlad Tepes, which translates as Vlad the Impaler. It's ironic that Vlad's favorite method of killing—staking a person through the heart—became known as the best way to dust a vampire!

Why wasn't the vampire working?

He was on his coffin break.

Little People

If you saw a person the size of a mouse riding a snail, would you freak out? You've just seen a piskie. In the legend of the Cornwall area of England, they are tiny creatures who could be good or bad.

What's a monster's favorite cheese?
Monster-ella.

What do you call a 10-foot monster?
Shorty.

How can you tell if a Martian is a good gardener?
It has a green thumb.

What kind of coffee does a vampire drink?
De-coffin-ated.

What do you get when a ghost sits on a branch?
Petrified wood.

What's a monster's favorite drink?
Ghoul-ade.

What did one ghost say to the other?
Don't spook until you're spoken to!

What's Dracula's favorite fruit?
Neck-tarine.

What's a ghost's favorite dessert?
Boo-berries and I-scream.

What kind of mistakes do ghosts make?
Boo-boos.

What do you call a witch that lives on the beach?
A sand-witch.

What's a vampire's favorite boat?
A blood vessel.

What do sea monsters eat for dinner?

Potato ships.

Why's the vampire so unpopular?
He's a pain-in-the-neck.

Who was the monster's date for the prom?
His ghoul-friend.

What type of dog do vampires have?
Blood hounds.

Why didn't the skeleton go to the party?
Because no body would go with him.

How do you know when a monster has a cold?
He starts coffin.

What do vampires take for bad colds?
Coffin drops.

Why do skeletons play the piano?
Because they don't have organs.

A Dose of Blood

Some scientists believe that back in the middle ages "vampires" were just sick people who had an incurable genetic disease called porphyria. This disease had unpleasant physical effects, such as the inability to tolerate sunlight. Back then they believed that drinking enough blood might help cure their symptoms.

Monster Madness

MEGA MOUNTAIN MAN

Ever heard of Kaptar, Biabin-guli, Grendel, Ferla Mohir, Brenin Ilwyd, Ngoloko, Kikomba, Gin-sung, Yeti, Mirygdy, Mecheny, the Chinese Wildman, Nguoi Rung, the Abominable Snowman, **Bigfoot,** or Sasquatch?

All these names have been given to a creature that lives in mountainous countries all over the world—or so people say. In the highest mountains in the world, the Himalayas, the Tibetans call him **Yeti**. In North America, he's called Bigfoot or Sasquatch. This mountain mystery is supposed to be big—up to twice the height of a man—and hairy, like a cross between a very large ape and human. Such big guys must have very large feet, and people claim to have found giant footprints left in the snow.

Some scientists believe that Bigfoot is a supposedly extinct primate called *Gigantopithecus Blacki.* "Blacky" lived in Asia about 300,000 years ago, and might have walked to other parts of the world when Asia was still joined to the North American continent.

MORE MONSTERS

The **Ninki Nanka,** as the people around the Gambia River call it, is said to be a monster the size of small dinosaur. It only appears at night, emerging from the ooze and slime of the mangrove swamps. It eats whatever it sees.

● ● ●

Back in the 1800s, the **Jago-nini**, which means "giant diver," was supposed to be lurking around. It was described a dinosaur-like creature with footprints the size of a dinner plate.

● ● ●

In 1992, scientists searched western Nepal for what they had been told were "giant elephants" that had two very large lumps on the forehead. These bumps were known to be on an extinct species of primitive elephant called **Stegodont**. Were these elephants descendants of the extinct elephant? Or, because they lived in an isolated area, did they mutate from interbreeding?

Underwater Elephants?

Elephants use their trunks as water hoses, food gatherers, and even props. But how about as a snorkel? Australian embryologists believe the elephant was once an aquatic animal that moved onto the land. If that's true, then the elephant's trunk may have evolved from a built-in snorkel.

Are You My Mummy?

Mummies aren't found only in Egypt. They're all over the world. In an Italian city called Palermo, for instance, there's an underground city of the dead that has about 6,000 bodies all amazingly well preserved by the cool, dry underground air. Over 100 years ago, when people died, their bodies were laid out on shelves in the clothes they were buried in. People who lived in Palermo would go down to the catacombs to pay respects to their dead relatives.

Where is ghosts' mail delivered?
The ghost office.

What does the ghost read every day?
His horror-scope.

What's the scariest ride at the amusement park?
The roller-ghoster.

What do ghosts eat for dinner?
Spook-ghetti.

Why did the 1000-year-old Egyptian go on the school field trip?
She heard that the mummies and daddies were invited, too.

Why did the mummy keep his bandages in the refrigerator?
He wanted to use them for cold cuts.

What happened when the toddler mummy told a lie?
He was sent to his tomb.

What does a witch order when she stays in a hotel?
Broom service.

Is it true that witches are afraid of dead bodies?
Of corpse it is.

How do you make a witch itch?
Take out the W.

Why did the vampire sit on the pumpkin?
He wanted to play squash.

What do you call twin boy vampires?
Blood brothers!

What do you say to a skeleton going on vacation?
Bone voyage!

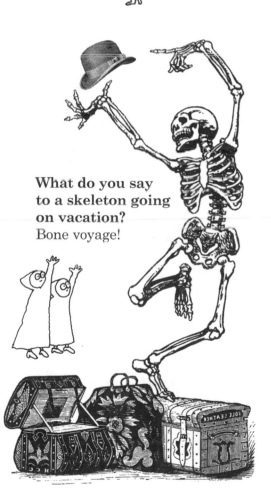

Why do elves get indigestion?
They keep goblin their food.

What do you get when you cross a cow with a werewolf?
A steak that bites back!

Ancient Wonders

DIG THIS!

As more and more archeology is done, we understand more about people who lived thousands of years ago. Or do we? We might be digging up hoaxes—or evidence that the past is still full of mysteries.

In the early 1960s stones were discovered in **Ica**, Peru. On them were carved images of dinosaurs, like triceratops and stegosaurus, with people hunting them and even flying on the backs of pterodons. The stone is an extremely hard mineral that would be difficult to carve with primitive tools. But the carvings are old—they are covered with a natural varnish, made by bacteria over thousands of years. Dinosaurs are said to have died out around 65 million years ago, but does this discovery show that they were still alive when humans were around 2 million years ago?

• • •

Archeologists in **Costa Rica** have discovered thousands of granite stone balls, ranging from the size of a tennis ball to as high as two men and weighing 16,000 kg (16 tons)—the combined weight of two large elephants! And they are absolutely perfect spheres. Some scientists think that an ancient war-like people called the Chibcha had slaves make the balls to create fort-like structures around their towns. But how did they make them so perfectly? Why are they round and not square? And how did they move them from the quarries where they were made?

• • •

Monuments from the Stone Age were built long before even the pyramids, and **Newgrange** in Ireland is one of the grandest. Newgrange is a huge mound with a passage inside that leads to a tomb in the center. No light ever gets all the way in, except for one morning in the year. On the winter solstice—the day with the shortest day and the longest night—the dawn sunlight streams in through a slot above the entrance. Did the ancients understand the Sun and the stars? Carvings inside the passage represent a sundial, calendars, and a map of the heavens.

Mad as a Hatter
Why would someone who makes hats be crazier than anyone else, as this phrase suggests? In the 19th century, when felt hats were very popular, a poisonous chemical called nitrate of mercury was used in making felt. Working with the chemical for years caused brain damage to many hat-makers.

Archeologists have dug up a small clay vessel that contains a copper cylinder held in place by asphalt. According to experts, if it had been filled with acid it might produce an electrical charge. What is amazing is that this thing—which might have been a battery—was made about 2,000 years ago, between 248 B.C. and 226 A.D.!

history
history
history

Can you guess the familiar saying?

Answer:
History repeats itself.

The Mystery of Animal Feelings

Some scientists believe that animals have feelings—others don't. It's not an easy question. Animal emotions are much more difficult to figure out than our own, because animals can't tell us how they are feeling. But they do communicate—watch for their body language.

SORRY SIGHT

If a **dog** has been bad, it might turn its head sideways and show its neck. It might even crouch down, wag its tail slowly, and lift its front paw to show you it is sorry. These are all things a wolf or wild dog might do. These wild relatives of our pets live in groups, with a boss, or Alpha, dog heading the pack. Pack members use these actions to show they recognize the leadership of the Alpha dog—for your pet, that's you. Later it may "smile" at you with its mouth wide open and its tongue out—this says, "I want to play now."

I'M THE BOSS!

Except for lions, the wild relatives of your house cat don't usually live in groups. But when they do, there is usually an Alpha cat. Homes with multiple cats will resemble a pride of lions, with the Alpha cat as king. Don't put another cat's food down first, because the Alpha cat will glower at you, growl, or shove the other cat out of the way—the Alpha lion always eats first and gets the most attention. And if you are caught stroking another cat, the Alpha cat might look away, avoiding eye contact when you look at it, to show it is jealous and angry.

Raining Cats and Dogs

This phrase, which means that it is raining really hard, might come from the fact that small animals sometimes lived in the straw roofs of medieval houses. When there was a heavy rain, the straw would get soaked and collapse, and fall into the house!

SO SAD

In Tanzania scientists studying **chimpanzee** behavior witnessed the death of a 50-year-old female chimpanzee. For days afterwards, the chimpanzee's son sat beside her lifeless body, holding her hand and whimpering. As the days went on, he withdrew from the other chimpanzees, and refused food and help from them. When he died three weeks later, some believe it was from grief.

• • •

There are many incidents of **elephants** trying to revive dying members of their herd, or standing by a dead friend for days. They've been seen gently touching the dead body with their trunks, hoping that the animal will somehow survive.

What do monkeys eat for dessert?

Chocolate chimp cookies.

**What has webbed feet
and wants to suck your
blood?**
Count Quack-ula.

**What's big, green, and
can't stop crying?**
The Incredible Sulk.

**What do vampires say
after they have eaten?**
Fang-you very much.

**What was written on
the robot's tombstone?**
Rust in peace.

**What do you call a
cat that's a ghost?**
A scaredy-cat.

**What room doesn't have
a ghost in it?**
A living room.

**How can you tell when
a mummy is angry?**
It flips its lid.

**What happened
when the girl ghost
met the boy ghost?**
It was love at first fright.

**What did the ghost have
for lunch?**
Grave-y.

That music's so loud it could wake the dead!

Want to Boo-gie?

What types of streets do ghosts live on?

Dead ends.

NO EXIT

What Big Eyes You've Got!

Real monsters lurk in the depths of the ocean. Although rarely seen, sometimes giant squids get caught in fishing nets or wash up on shore so we can get a close-up view of these gigantic creatures. Their eyes alone are the size of a car's hubcaps—the largest eyes in the world!

Knock!
Knock!

Another joke? I thought the book was over!

I must have been mistaken!

Knock!
Knock!
Knock!